D1560652

RADIO CONTROL
AIRPLANE
Finishing
& Detailing

Contents

CHAPTER 4

Adding the finer details

Group Editor-in-Chief Tom Atwood
Editors Gerry Yarrish, Debra Sharp
Assistant Editor Bob Hastings
Copy Director Lynne Sewell
Senior Copyeditor Molly O'Byrne
Corporate Art Director Betty Nero
Assistant Art Director Alessandra Cirillo
Staff Photographer Walter Sidas
Director of Operations David Bowers
Production Associates Chris Hoffmaster, Tom Hurley
Director of Circulation Ned Bixler
Circulation Assistant P.J. Uva

President and CEO Michael F. Doyle
Vice President G.E. DeFrancesco
Group Publishers L.V. DeFrancesco,
Yvonne M. DeFrancesco

PRINTED IN THE USA

Copyright 1999© by Air Age Inc.   ISBN: 0-911295-51-8

All rights reserved, including the right of reproduction in whole or part or any form. This book, or parts thereof, may not be reproduced or transmitted in any form by any means without the consent of the publisher.

Published by Air Age Inc., 100 East Ridge, Ridgefield, CT 06877-4606; (203) 431-9000; fax (203) 431-3000; www.airage.com.

Introduction

One of the "Master Modeler" series, *R/C Airplane Finishing and Detailing* is composed of some of the best "how-to" articles that have appeared in *Model Airplane News* magazine. Written by the pros, this publication is a collection of unique modeling secrets, hints and tips that cover everything from the basics to advanced techniques.

If you've ever had unanswered modeling questions about such things as working with dope and applying fabric covering, or achieving smooth resin and painted finishes, this photo-illustrated, four-chapter book will provide all the answers.

And when it comes to easy-to-do details, the pros hold nothing back. From riveting to lighting systems to dummy radial engines, *R/C Airplane Finishing and Detailing* is filled with the stuff that scale dreams are made of. It's a must-have modeling resource.

1

Finishing with fabric

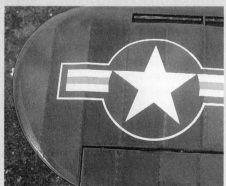

Finish models with dope

by Jim Sandquist

MATERIALS

To do a good job of covering a 6- to 8-foot-span airplane, here's what you'll need:

- 1 quart clear butyrate dope
- 1 pint clear nitrate dope
- 1 quart nitrate thinner
- 1 pint silver butyrate dope
- Colored butyrate dope for the final paint finish (your choice)
- 1 pint retarder
- Unscented talcum powder
- 1 can Sig Stix-It or Balsarite
- High-quality camel-hair paint brush at least 1 inch wide.
- Covering fabric (your choice)
- 400-grit wet-or-dry sandpaper
- Quart containers for mixing

There always seems to be one talented guy who continually shows up at competitions with beautiful, butyrate-dope-finished models. What a terrific way to finish a model! It always looks great, it never sags, it's impervious to fuel, and it's highly admired by other modelers. If you've ever looked at dope-finished models and thought, "Boy, I wish I could finish my planes like that," read on. I'll show you the technique I learned from an old-time modeler.

FULL-SIZE FINISHES

This finishing technique is the one that's used to cover full-scale aircraft. Although some of the dope-and-fabric-finish process is difficult to put into words, I'll try to take you from start to finish.

Several butyrate and nitrate dope products are available. Randolph Products* makes good dopes for the full-size aircraft industry, and Sig Mfg. Co.* provides a complete line of nitrate and butyrate dopes in a variety of colors. Sig's products are probably the most readily available and are bottled in small quantities that are convenient for smaller modeling projects. They're available directly from Sig and at most hobby stores.

This process is not much more difficult than other means of finishing, and the cost is close to that of the average iron-on coverings. Remember, high-quality workmanship usually takes a little extra effort, and you'll find that this is worth the time.

MIXING TECHNIQUE

Before you start to cover the airframe, you need to make three different dope formulas—approximately 1 quart each—mixed to a brushing consistency so that they can be brushed onto the airframe and the covering material. In another container, mix clear butyrate dope and thinner to a ratio of approximately 60-percent dope and 40-percent thinner. Stir vigorously until well mixed. Keep in mind that this ratio is approximate; some brands of butyrate may be slightly thicker than others. You want a mixture that's slightly thicker than straight thinner. In another container, mix the nitrate dope and nitrate thinner in the same way.

In a third container, mix butyrate dope and butyrate thinner as described, but first add some unscented talcum powder—approximately 1 inch of powder on the bottom of the 1-quart container—for 1 quart of mixed dope and thinner. This will be used for the filler (or base coat). Unscented talcum powder isn't usually available off the shelf, but it can be ordered. One bottle of it costs around $7 and contains enough powder for several models. Don't use scented talcum powder; in some cases, the fragrance in the powder will forever adhere to the aircraft. Set your mixtures aside and prepare the airframe for covering.

PREPARING THE AIRFRAME

An old adage says that, "Your finish is only as good as what's underneath." This really holds true when covering and painting an aircraft. Make sure that your airframe has been well-sanded and that all nicks and dings have been filled. Double-check to ensure that the wing, the tail surfaces and the landing gear all fit well. When you're satisfied that they do, brush one coat of nitrate dope over the entire airframe, and let it dry for about half an hour. When it has dried, sand the airframe to a smooth finish with 320-grit sandpaper. Once this is complete, you can begin to cover your model.

COVERING MATERIALS

For many years, models have been covered with silk, Japanese tissue and silkspan. Although these coverings are still used, newer, easier to use and stronger products have, for the most part, replaced them. Sig Koverall and Coverite's* Super Coverite are the best of the new coverings. Because all fabric coverings have a weave, some shrink more in one direction than another, so pay attention to the direction of the weave when you apply the fabric to your model. Which covering should you use? That really depends on you.

• **Super Coverite** is a cloth that's applied like any other iron-on covering. There's a heat-activated adhesive on the covering's back, so application with a covering iron is simple. Unlike other iron-on coverings, however, Super Coverite doesn't have a painted finish. It can easily be applied with no wrinkles, and it shrinks very tightly, so it's the perfect surface for a painted finish. Because it has adhesive already applied to it, you can cut it with a scissors or a hobby knife without its fraying. Coverite offers a brush-on adhesive—Balsarite— that dries in minutes and delivers great results.

• **Sig Koverall** cloth is similar to Super Coverite, but it doesn't come with an adhesive on the back of it; you must apply heat-activated adhesive to the structure before you cover it. Koverall tends to fray when it's cut; but that can be prevented by brushing on a light coat of dope and letting it dry before you cut it. Koverall is less expensive because it has no adhesive. Sig offers an adhesive—Stix-It—that dries in minutes and gives good results.

The choice is yours; they both work well. I prefer Sig Koverall; Sig manufactures everything for the covering process, and there's no question about compatibility of all the necessary materials. I will discuss the application of Sig Koverall throughout the rest of this article.

Randolph Products has provided dope for the aviation industry for years. Check your local airport for a dealer.

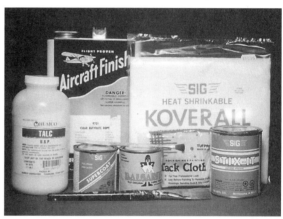

The products you'll need to do a good job include: your choice of dope, Sig Koverall, a tack cloth, adhesive and a camel-hair brush.

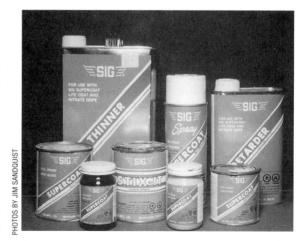

PHOTOS BY JIM SANDQUIST

Sig dopes are readily available through most hobby shops and directly from the manufacturer. Sig provides everything you need to achieve a great finish.

APPLYING FABRIC

Now that your airframe has been prepped with a coat of nitrate dope, it's time to cover the wing. Brush a coat of heat-activated adhesive onto the trailing edge and the wingtips, and set the wing aside to dry. Meanwhile, cut out a piece of covering that's large enough to be wrapped all the way around the wing. Once the glue has dried, use your hobby iron to stick the fabric into place where you applied the glue.

Remove any large wrinkles by adjusting the material as you iron it into place. Apply another light coat of adhesive over the fabric-covered trailing edge. When it has dried, iron the overlapping covering material down, and trim the edge. Once all the edges have been ironed down and sealed, apply heat to the covering; work from the center outward to remove all the wrinkles and to uni-

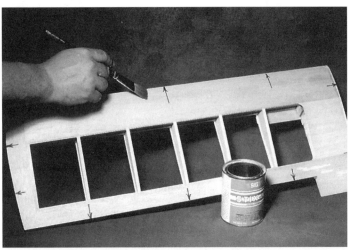

Apply your adhesive (Stix-It or Balsarite) to the perimeter of the wing, as shown by the arrows on the wing in the photograph.

When applying the dope to the fabric, always brush in the same direction, and keep the coats thin to minimize brush marks.

formly tighten the covering material. This process is used on all the other parts of the airframe, including the fuselage, stab, fin, elevators and rudder. Keep all seams as straight as possible, and make all overlaps uniform in width. You'll be amazed at how forgiving fabric covering is; it goes around compound curves easily, and it produces a very strong, tight covering job.

PROPERTIES OF DOPE

Nitrate and butyrate dope each have distinct properties. Dope finishes are used on full-scale, fabric-covered aircraft because dope remains flexible and resists cracking. It takes weeks—even months—for dope to cure fully. But don't worry, you won't have to wait that long to fly your model; dope-finished surfaces dry to the touch very quickly.

Fumes from dope and dope thinners are another consideration; they have been known to cause dizziness and headaches. I suggest that you paint your model outdoors or, at the very least, in a well-ventilated room, and wear a snug-fitting respirator paint mask with replaceable filters.

APPLYING DOPE

Use your camel-hair brush to apply a very light coat of nitrate dope to the covering; make sure that it doesn't soak all the way through the weave or fall through to the other side of your wing. Also, be sure to always brush in the same direction and keep the coats very thin. The goal is to fill the fabric weave and allow the fabric's weave to show slightly through your final finish.

Recall that you applied a coat of nitrate dope to your airframe before you covered it. New coats of both butyrate and nitrate dope melt slightly into previously applied coats. Because you applied nitrate to your airframe and are now applying a light coat to the fabric, the fabric will bond to the wooden airframe very firmly. Nitrate dope also sticks to fabric better than butyrate does. This light application of nitrate dope will seal the fabric and provide a good foundation for the butyrate base coat. This is the last step in which you'll use nitrate dope; butyrate will be used for the rest of the finish.

Butyrate dope bonds well to nitrate and gives your model a good fuelproof finish; nitrate dope isn't fuelproof.

Remember, you can apply butyrate over nitrate, but you should not apply nitrate over butyrate! Next, brush on two coats of butyrate dope, allowing ample drying time between coats. When these have dried, lightly sand with 400-grit wet-or-dry sandpaper. Don't sand through the fabric; just remove the brush marks. Now, apply three more coats of butyrate, lightly sanding between each coat.

By this time, you should have a smooth finish. If you hold the model up to the light, you should see the fabric's weave beginning to fill in. For the remaining base coats, use the butyrate and talcum powder mix. It acts as a filler and gives a very uniform base. Be sure to stir it very well before and while you apply it. Keep the coats as thin as possible. If the mixture doesn't flow well, or it cakes up when you brush it, add more thinner. Brush on three or four coats, and continue to sand lightly between them. You're looking for a uniformly built-up finish that has a slight sheen. After you have achieved this, you're ready to start spraying.

SPRAYING DOPE

Many modelers are hesitant to spray-paint their models; they either don't have the facilities to paint, or they think they need expensive equipment. Because the dope mixture is thin, it can be applied with only about 25psi of air pressure. This means that you can apply it with one of the smaller hobby sprayers. If you don't have spray equipment, Sig sells dope in aerosol spray cans. For the best possible finish, wipe a clean tack cloth over the model before applying each coat of dope to remove any surface dust.

Painting with Compressors

If you've been in this hobby for any time, you've done some painting. If you're like most of us, you usually reach for a can of spray paint. The more painting you do, the more you find yourself wishing you owned a compressor. There are many options.

• Possibly the most affordable hobby compressor setup is from K.J. Miller Corp*. Their Model 2000 puts out a constant 20psi and comes with an airbrush, a 1-pint spray bottle, a 1-quart spray bottle and an air hose, and it costs less than $200 (complete).

• Badger Air-Brush Co.* makes a number of small hobby compressors that start at around $150; that doesn't include an airbrush, paint bottles, or a hose. Plan to spend an additional $50 to $100 on these items. Good, artist-quality airbrushes run from $35 to well over $200; if you decide to buy one of these, buy one with a medium tip, and buy a large paint bottle.

• If you have space in your workshop, it might be best to invest in a small commercial compressor. These are available in most home-improvement stores. I have a 2.5hp compressor that will supply 90psi at 5 cubic feet per minute. Units like this cost approximately $175 to $225, plus the cost of the hose, the water trap and a medium-size spray gun. Expect to pay between $250

K.J. Miller Corp. of Elkhart, IN, makes good spray-painting equipment that's used by many modelers.

and $300 for a complete setup.

• Commercial spray guns—often called "touchup guns"—are relatively inexpensive ($30 to $50) and are available from many sources. Automotive painting outlets, hobby shops and department stores carry them. Many mail-order catalogs carry them, too, and these guns are very useful for spraying the clear buildup coats.

The important thing to remember is that once you've invested in this equipment, you'll be set for many more projects. If you're starting from scratch, check the classified ads in your local paper; they're filled with all kinds of inexpensive treasures. Good hunting and happy spraying!

Left: air compressors such as this are available at hardware stores and home-improvement centers. They provide more than enough air pressure to paint model aircraft. Right: the Badger Air-Brush Co. compressor is perfect for applying dope finishes.

Another advantage of spraying on dope is that it dries very quickly, so you can do it either in a garage or outdoors without worrying about excessive overspray. Dope dries so quickly that the overspray is generally dry before it hits the ground, and that makes cleanup easy. A temperature of 70 to 80 degrees with low humidity is ideal for spraying. High humidity can cause "blushing" (discussed later).

FINISHING

• **A silver lining.** Because colored dopes are translucent, before applying them, you must cover the entire model with a very light coat of silver dope to prevent the wood grain from showing through. Generally, two very light coats of silver are enough. Silver isn't a forgiving color, though, and it will reveal most of the imperfections in your base coats. Now is the time to touch up areas that you aren't satisfied with.

• **Applying color.** As is the case with most paints, you apply the lightest color first and put the darker colors over them. Again, keep the paint thin—only slightly thicker than the thinner. Spray it on evenly, and be sure to apply it slightly wet; a dry finish doesn't always bond well. A pressure of 20 to 30psi is adequate; any more than that tends to result in a dry finish and produce more overspray. The best results are achieved by applying many light coats, as opposed to spraying on only a few heavy coats. Runs or dust can be wet-sanded out at any time. Minor scratches caused by sanding will disappear when the final clearcoat is applied.

When you've completed the base color, let the aircraft dry for 24 hours before you mask for the other colors. I use 3M™ vinyl Fine Line Masking Tapes that can be found in every automotive-supply store. When you remove masking tape, slowly pull it back over itself at a low angle to the surface to prevent the paint from being lifted off. When you remove the tape, you may notice that some flashing or paint comes off with it. Don't worry about this; wet-sanding with 400-grit wet-or-dry sandpaper will fix it.

• **Final clearcoat.** When you get to this point, you may notice that some colors look milky, or "blushed." This was caused by high humidity when the dope was applied. It can be prevented either by waiting for a very dry day to paint or by adding a small amount of retarder to the dope (available from Sig and Randolph). Blushing disappears when clear dope is applied over it. If you paint on a humid day, add retarder to your clearcoat. The clearcoat—a mixture of clear butyrate dope and butyrate thinner mixed 1:4—should be applied with 20 to 30psi. Applied in thin, uniform, wet coats, the clearcoat really makes your finish shine!

CONCLUSION

Painting always takes a little more effort than using an iron-on finish, but I think the result is always better. If you've ever painted with enamel or polyurethane, I think you'll like working with dope. It has a very short drying time, remains flexible and is very easy to work with. Touchup and repair work are also easy. If you're up to the challenge of something new, I suggest you try this technique—but on a small model first. There's no substitute for actually doing it yourself. Good luck!

Addresses are listed alphabetically in the Index of Manufacturers on page 146.   ✦

Secrets to covering with fabric

by Dave Platt, with illustrations by Jim Newman

After many years of building scale models, I've come up with various methods for the covering and finishing process. The one that you choose depends on your model. Although what is given here are step-by-step suggestions, I don't intend to imply that these are the only ones that work. Variations can be made without risking disaster, and if you've developed techniques that work well for you, it may be best to continue with them. If, however, your experience is limited, or covering and finishing have always given you a hard time, I suggest that you follow these steps without modification. You'll be starting out with a proven method, and you can devote your attention entirely to improving your skill level.

Here we see a colorful de Havilland Tigermoth. It's typical of a fabric-covered aircraft and will present the modeler with much surface detail to duplicate. Photo courtesy of Scale Model Research.

MATERIALS

I've been involved with model building for many years, and I've seen more "new and miraculous" ways of covering and finishing a model than there are P-51 kits on the market. A few of these have stood the test of time; many haven't. Some have useful applications in other areas of modeling, but they don't give good results on scale models.

• **Plastic films.** Super MonoKote* is extremely useful as a parting film for making fillets, fiberglass landing-gear doors, etc. Other than this, films

Rag wings are full of details, such as rib stitching and pinked tape. The larger your model, the more important these details become to the appearance of the model.

should be avoided for covering a scale model. Plastic film invariably wrinkles and lifts off the model's surface. I feel that Mylar imparts a "toy-like" look to a scale model. Plastic does have a good gloss (perhaps too good), but if you're reproducing a glossy subject, there are better ways, as you shall see.

• **Silkspan (a rag paper).** Probably the oldest and most traditional of all coverings, silkspan is still very useful to scale modelers. It's light, easy to work with, resilient and inexpensive. On the minus side, it is, of course, weaker than nylon and requires the use of dopes, which I prefer to avoid. I use silkspan on fabric-covered control surfaces.

• **Silk.** Silk is useful mainly when applied over a base layer of silkspan. Silk alone does not do an entirely satisfactory covering job. This is because its open weave allows too much dope to soak through; this forms drops of dried dope on the inside of the silk. Needless to say, the appearance is terrible.

• **Nylon.** Nylon, which has none of the problems of silk, has a close weave that prevents dopes or paints from penetrating too far. Dacron and other man-made fibers fall into this category. For covering a fabric-covered model, polyester is very suitable. This is sold at fabric stores as a lining material; it's inexpensive and very strong.

• **Carl Goldberg* Coverite.** This is a man-made fiber with an adhesive backing; it's heat-shrinkable and should be ironed on. It's expensive, but when you follow the directions that are supplied, it's also a fine product that will produce very good results.

Although its manufacturer suggests that you don't use nitrate dope on Coverite, my experience indicates that this isn't a problem.

• **Sig* Koverall.** This uncoated, heat-shrinkable polyester fabric has no adhesive and is not expensive. To stick it to a model, you can use dope in the traditional silk-and-dope method, or you can use Sig's Stix-It heat-activated adhesive.

• **F&M Enterprises*.** This company has a product called "Stits Lite Covering," which is very similar to full-size-aircraft covering material. The material is glued to the model with a heat-activated adhesive called "Poly Tak."

THE COVERING PROCESS

The covering material you have chosen will be one of two kinds: iron-on, heat-shrinkable (Coverite) or one of these fabrics: silkspan, polyester, silk, or nylon. In the early stages of covering, the methods vary somewhat. For Coverite, follow the detailed instructions supplied with the material. An imperfect covering job with this product is almost always the result of not reading or following the instructions. Take special care with the grain direction, or a loose covering job can result. Once you have the ship covered and are ready for finishing, switch from the manufacturer's instructions to those described here. For silkspan, polyester, silk and nylon, proceed as follows:

1 Sand the airframe very carefully at all points of covering contact. Use 220-grit aluminum-oxide paper. Fill any dings with a microballoons/K&B* resin mix (or vinyl-spackle paste), and sand out. Be very fussy with this job; the final appearance of the finished model depends on it.

2 Brush a coat of full-strength, clear nitrate dope over all areas where the covering will contact wood. Allow to dry.

3 Lightly sand off any "fuzz" with 220 sandpaper, and apply a second coat of clear. Allow to dry; then repeat the sanding.

4 Cut the covering material a little oversize. Soak it with water, and then squeeze out the excess (leave the material only damp). Now, working as quickly as possible, smooth out the damp material over the area to be covered. Gently tug out any wrinkles. Do not be particularly concerned to get the material drum-tight but be sure to get it smooth and wrinkle-free.

5 Brush a coat of nitrate dope onto the covering material, but only where it contacts the wood. As the damp material and the dope dry, the covering should adhere well and shrink fairly tightly.

6 Inspect the results. Any imperfections (wrinkles or obvious looseness) can be dampened and doped

again. Only when the job is perfect can you proceed. Do not expect later coats of dope to improve a problem area! The covering job will never be any better than it is right now. If, in spite of extra attention, problems with wrinkles remain, remove the covering material, and try again. You may have areas of blushed (white) dope. Do not be concerned; this is a normal reaction of dope and water.

The following steps apply to the fabric covering, and they should be followed after the Coverite has been applied according to manufacturer's instructions.

7 Brush—or better yet, spray—a coat of thinned, clear dope over the completely covered model. As this coat dries, the covering should gain a little tightness and some of the blushed effect will disappear. Lightly sand the entire model with 220 paper.

8 If you're double-covering (silkspan), this is the time to apply the second layer of material. Wet the material and cover, using an overall coat of clear as adhesive.

9 Now apply three or four more coats of clear (use spray if possible). The last coat should be well-thinned (25 percent dope, 75 percent thinner).

PRIMING

The covering and clear doping having been completed, lightly sand the model in preparation for priming. The primer must be sprayed on for the best results. When the primer is dry (two hours for Du Pont no. 100S; overnight for K&B), sand very carefully. It is advantageous to use 220- and 320-grit silicon-carbide wet or dry sandpaper on the primer. Use it wet to prevent the paper from becoming clogged. Remember, the surface quality you're now seeing represents the quality of the final job; the color coats will not correct surface imperfections. If there are any flaws, attend to them now with extra primer or filler, and sand them out.

SURFACE DETAILS

By now, the model should be looking great. At this time, add surface details, such as rib stitching and tapes, as required.
• **Rib stitches.** These are best represented by Elmer's white glue applied in thin lines across each rib at a suitable spacing. The glue is applied with a hypodermic needle.

This is a sample of Clearprint 1000H draftsman's vellum that has been pulled up against the serrated strip of a Saran Wrap box. Place it next to a full-size sample of 2-inch-wide pinking tape and count the points; the strip of vellum is almost exactly ¼ scale!

• **Rib tapes.** A number of methods have evolved. My favorite uses the serrated cutter from a wax-paper or plastic-wrap package to cut strips of paper (tracing vellum). The strips are soaked in water

until they become limp and are doped down over the glue "stitches." An additional coat or two of clear dope will make the paper ready for color.

Below is the process of duplicating rib stitching and pinked taped as mentioned in the text. Illustrator Jim Newman gives credit for the original idea in 1973 to Keith Ward of Elmhurst, IL.

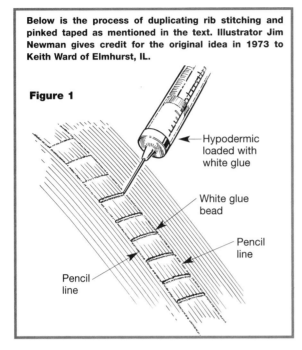

Figure 1

Hypodermic loaded with white glue

White glue bead

Pencil line

Pencil line

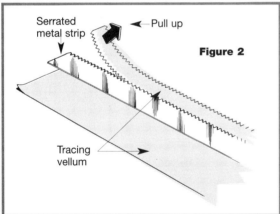

Serrated metal strip

Pull up

Figure 2

Tracing vellum

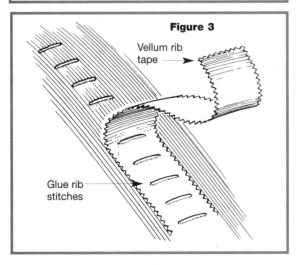

Figure 3

Vellum rib tape

Glue rib stitches

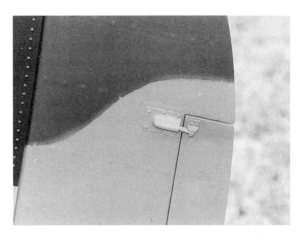

This close-up of the rudder on Sepp Uberlacher's Tempest shows that fabric covering is also required for heavy-metal warbirds. Many WW II fighters and bombers had fabric-covered control surfaces.

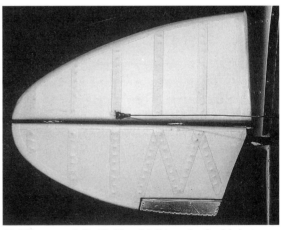

Stabilizers need rib-stitching detail to make the fabric covering look correct.

PAINTING

When you have the colors you need, paint the model. For the best effect of realism pay close attention to the degree of gloss you need. Many full-size aircraft have matte or satin finishes. In these cases, use the satin part B. Even in cases where the prototype is "glossy," it's unwise to use straight gloss part B. Very few full-size subjects have the rich, deep gloss that model epoxy paints normally have. A much more convincing effect is produced by dulling the shine to some degree by premixing the gloss hardener with 10- to 20-percent satin hardener.

Covering a scale model can be as pleasant as any job that our hobby has to offer. Using this process will at least get you started in the right direction for a good-looking, successful covering job. Good luck.

Addresses are listed alphabetically in the Index of Manufacturers on page 146.

Covering and finishing scale models

by Dave Platt, with illustrations by Jim Newman

It could be true to say that a percentage of scale modelers may subconsciously be artists; they love to paint, and a scale model provides an opportunity to follow this desire. The airframe itself becomes, in effect, a three-dimensional canvas. On this base, the builder can find satisfaction in creating what may be called, in every respect, a work of art.

So why is it true that, for another modeler, this is a hated chore? The poor fellow's experience makes him foresee the ruination of his finely made airframe, and he dreads every minute of it. I believe there are three ways for the guys in the second category to place themselves among those in the first. These are:
• modify expectations;
• learn techniques of preparation;
• choose the right materials.

EXPECTATION

It is very unfortunate that covering and finishing are often regarded as less important stages in model building. The feeling is: "OK, the model is built; let's get it covered, and we can fly it tomorrow!" To some extent, members of the model trade encourage this attitude. They advertise materials as instant answers. Many things today are designed to produce quick results, and sometimes they work; but, by and large, there's no free lunch. Rapid methods often lead to miserable conse-

Dave Platt, the master of scale-model finishing and painting, poses with one of his projects—the Grumman Mohawk. The Mohawk—typical of models covered with fiberglass cloth—has numerous surface details such as rivets, screws and panel lines.

quences, and the trusting modeler thinks it's his fault. Let's set the matter straight with a few home truths.
• Covering and finishing are major stages of model building.
• It takes as long to do a good job on the exterior as it does to build the airframe. A model that has been built—with the engine and radio installed—is estimated to be 50 percent complete.
• The above estimate applies to experienced builders.
• The pleasure derived from the finish is directly proportional to the quality of work done.

The engine nacelle is full of details; the separation line for the removable portion of the cowl is barely visible.

The aft portion of the engine nacelle is dominated by the large, scale exhaust duct. Notice all the smaller details on the model: raised panels, air scoops, antennas, etc.; they all add up to a beautifully executed model.

Although you may spend more time on perfecting your finish, the result will be better, and you'll enjoy doing it more.

If you've always had nightmares about covering and finishing, you might be saying something like this now: "Wow! No wonder I've never done too well! If it takes experts a while, I didn't have a chance of a good result in the time I spent!" True! And all because nobody told you what to expect. My hope is that I'll convince you that the trick is to slow down. This is the way of the experts.

Before I go into a blow-by-blow account of the techniques used to cover and finish a scale model, I'll explain one other important thing. I'm not necessarily referring to a rich, deep, 20-coat gloss. The true art of scale modeling is to "Tell it like it is." In seeking to model a full-size subject, we should contrive to reproduce that subject as it really looks—good, bad, or indifferent.

Indeed, convincingly copying the scruffy look of a well-used plane can be much more difficult than getting a smooth, glossy finish. Of course, if our subject aircraft is indeed clean, bright and shiny, we want our model to be so, but we might be modeling, say, a combat warplane with a victory tally or mission count to its name. If this is the case, it's obvious that the plane didn't get these credentials overnight; it took time, and time takes a toll on the outside of an airframe.

With this in mind, remember that the convincingly battered and very dirty scale model can have a trophy-winning finish.

All right then; let's proceed. It has been said that you can't make a silk purse out of a sow's ear; neither can you get a beautiful finish on a roughly

The forward portion of the fuselage shows many great details. Note the subtle windshield-wiper marks on the clear windshield. Rivets, panel lines, access hatches and other details add to the overall authenticity of Dave's Mohawk.

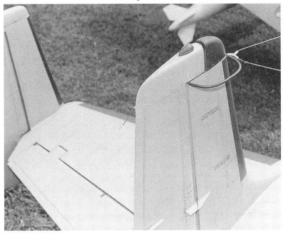

The center fin and rudder are equally detailed. Notice the small anti-static-wand wire trailing from the rudder's trailing edge.

built airframe. That's why I'll begin with preparation techniques.

PREPARATION TECHNIQUES

The essential difference between a poor model and a great one can be summed up in one word—sandpaper! There has never been a ding in an airframe that couldn't be filled and sanded level, or a protruding spar that couldn't be sanded flush. One horror sometimes encountered on totally sheeted subjects is what I call the "starved-horse" look: sheeting sags between the ribs in a wing or the bulkheads in a fuselage and produces an undulating surface.

There are a number of defenses against this. Two are obvious: use more ribs or bulkheads to shorten the unsupported span; or use firmer wood for the skins.

Other solutions that may not be as well-known but are equally important in sag prevention are to

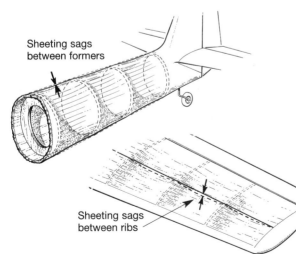

Sheeting sags between formers

Sheeting sags between ribs

For a great-looking model, avoid some common problems. The "starved horse" look is caused by sheeting that sags between formers or ribs and produces undulating surfaces. To prevent this, use thicker covering material or install more ribs or formers.

use only curing-type finishing products, i.e., where possible, avoid materials that dry by evaporating (more on this later), and to sand all skins thoroughly after joining them and cutting them to size, but before attaching them to the model.

Sanding the skins when they're in place must be held to a minimum. Never join skins on a wing, for example. (What happens is this: naturally, you have to sand the joints. Between the ribs, the sanding block presses the sheeting down, and the area supported by a rib is sanded very thin. These thinned areas then show later as depressions that give the model a rippled appearance. Obviously, strength is affected, too.)

Prior to covering, break down the model into as many individual components as possible. Remove

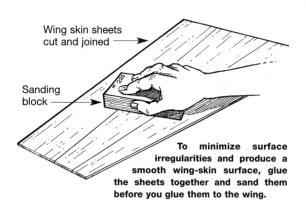

To minimize surface irregularities and produce a smooth wing-skin surface, glue the sheets together and sand them before you glue them to the wing.

the engine, radio, servos, horns, hinges, links, etc. Mask off the window areas (but not the frames) with tape. Finally, using 220-grit sandpaper, lightly hand-sand the component you're about to cover. Get it really smooth! Ready? Lay the part down on a foam pad or a similar soft surface (watch out for loose pins that will ding the weak, bare balsa), and you're ready to start.

METHODS

Over many years of building scale models, modelers have evolved a variety of methods for the covering and finishing process. The one that's chosen will depend on the subject being modeled. Although I give detailed, step-by-step suggestions, I'm not implying that these are the only ones that work. Variations can be made without risking disaster, and if you have developed techniques that work well for you, it may be as well to continue with them. If, however, your experience is limited or you've always had a difficult time with covering/finishing, I suggest you follow my steps exactly. You'll be starting out with a proven method, and you'll be able to devote your atten-

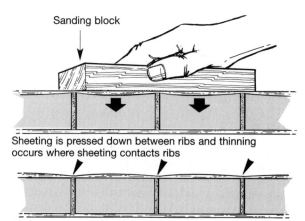

Sheeting is pressed down between ribs and thinning occurs where sheeting contacts ribs

Sheeting springs back up after sanding, leaving depressions over the top of each rib

This shows what happens if you sand your wing skins after you've glued them to your wing.

tion entirely to improving your skills.

CHOOSING MATERIALS

• **Fiberglass cloth.** Because it works well with resins to produce a strong and durable finish, glass cloth is the standard material for covering any all-sheeted airplane. Glass cloth is usually found in hobby shops in two weights: ¾ ounce per square yard and 2 ounces per square yard. Generally speaking, the 2-ounce cloth is useful for wings and fuselages of large (over 6-foot span) models. The ¾-ounce cloth is best used for empennages on these larger models and as an overall covering for smaller models. This technique is superior in every respect to any other method.

• **Paint.** Two manufacturers—Hobby Poxy* and K&B Manufacturing*—make excellent model paints that pass the most critical trials. Both companies make a full line of finishing products. Of the two, I prefer K&B's resin and primer, but I find the colors of both equally good. Because these seem to be the products of choice for most scale modelers, let's examine them in more detail.

K&B resin. This is a polyester resin and is not to be confused with (or used with) epoxy resins. I use this product with glass cloth to cover solid and sheeted areas. A second coat of resin will seal the cloth properly and make it ready for priming. The resin cures fast, is easy to sand, makes an excellent base for primer or paint and isn't affected by fuel. It smells a bit and may draw complaints from your family or pets, but it won't harm you.

K&B primer. This is a two-part white filler, which is

Tricks with MonoKote

FILLETS

Here's how to make a truly outstanding fillet that will fit so well, you'll hardly see the seam.

1 From the root rib to a little farther out than the width of the fillet, cover the wing's uncovered upper surface with MonoKote*. Firmly iron it down onto the bare balsa, and be careful to remove all air bubbles.

2 Mount the wing on the fuselage. Place a strip of masking tape on the fuselage at the upper line of the required fillet and also across the wing at the outer edge of the fillet. Make a small, thick batch of K&B resin and Prather phenolic microballoons.

3 Add hardener, and use an artist's spatula to trowel the mix into the wing/fuselage junction.

4 After 10 to 20 minutes, the microballoons will reach a "gel point," i.e., the mixture will have solidified but won't have cured fully. Later, it will get very hard, but at this point, it can be cut like soft cheese. Using a knife, coarse sandpaper, or even the blade of the spatula, pare away the microballoons to the approximate shape of the fillet.

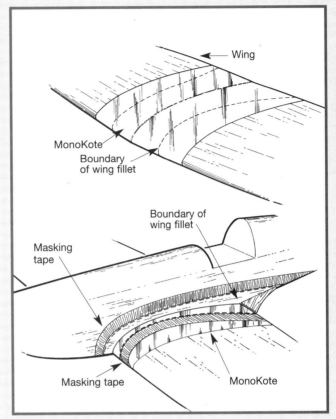

Fillets are easy to make using MonoKote as a barrier between the fuselage and the wing.

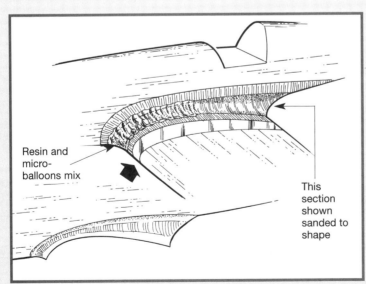

The wing can be easily separated from the finished fairing because of the MonoKote separation barrier.

5 When you get the feel of this, continue to mix more microballoons until you have both fillets roughed out.

6 Let the fillets harden completely (overnight is best), then sand them to their final shape and smoothness. Sand to the limits outlined by the masking tape; then remove the tape.

7 Now for the good part! Remove the screws that are holding the wing. With a helper holding the aft fuselage under the stab, stand the model on its nose. With the flat part of your palm, firmly rap both wings until they break free of the body.

8 Remove the MonoKote from the wings. You now have the best-fitting fillet you've ever seen.

applied after the resin has been sanded. I've found this to be the best primer on the model market.

K&B/Hobby Poxy colors. These consist of a paint color (part A) and a hardener (part B). Until mixed, the shelf life of part A seems indefinite while part B doesn't last quite as long. Once parts A and B have been combined, the paint will cure, even if you leave it in the can. In other words, it works just like epoxy glues.

The color (part A) comes only one way, but the hardener (part B) comes in two ways: a gloss and a matte (or satin). Depending on which hardener you use, your model will have either a glossy finish or a dull one. Either way, it will be fuelproof. There are a few things to note about this paint:

■ K&B SuperPoxy and Hobby Poxy paints can be mixed. You can use the color from one and the hardener from the other. The colors will mix freely—a handy attribute when you need a certain camouflage color and must mix one company's yellow with another's red, for instance. Though for the most part, I prefer to use K&B's satin hardener, I do

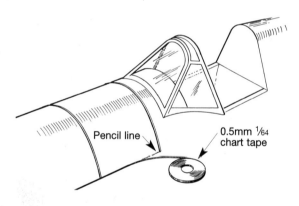

Panel lines can be duplicated with flexible 1/64-inch Formaline chart tape. For a raised panel line, leave the tape on; for a recessed panel line, remove the tape after priming but before painting.

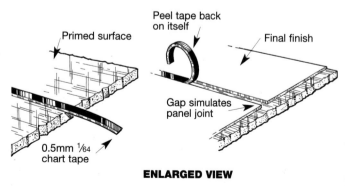

ENLARGED VIEW

find it necessary to extend my color range by including Hobby Poxy's Cub Yellow, Dark Blue and Maroon (part A), which K&B does not offer.

■ Mixed paint will keep for several days in a refrigerator.

■ Colors hardened with the matte part B will dry much faster on the model than those hardened with the gloss part B.

Thinners. Both brands work well, and you need not try any substitute; nothing else will work. I prefer the K&B thinner even when using Hobby Poxy paints.

Clear paint. Both Hobby Poxy and SuperPoxy make a clear paint that's used with a hardener just like the colors. The clear is used as a final coat over the color. I paint the model entirely, using only matte hardener. This makes use of the matte paint's faster drying referred to earlier. The final sheen is achieved with the clearcoat.

Before we leave the subject of paints, there is one more product I'd like to mention. Du Pont makes a one-part acrylic primer (no. 100S), which has given me good results. This gray filler dries very quickly. You must use silicon-carbide sandpaper with this primer, because it will soon load up aluminum-oxide paper.

A technique I use and recommend is to mix satin/matte hardener with thinner before mixing the hardener with part A. As supplied, satin part B is very thick and sludgy. This makes it difficult to stir to an even consistency, and this can lead to wide variations in sheen from one paint batch to another. Because we thin the paint before applying it anyway, I've found it an advantage to premix the satin hardener with an equal volume of thinner. Indeed, I usually keep a good quantity (1 quart or so) of this mix ready to be combined with any of the numerous typical model colors. The ratio, instead of one part color to one part hardener, is now, of course, changed to one part color to two parts mix. This gives a one-part-A to one-part-B to one-part-thinner final ratio, which is an ideal viscosity for spraying.

Naturally, that can of "mixed" part B will settle out fairly quickly, but a vigorous shaking is all that's needed to blend the "powder" back into the solution. While on the subject of settling, I should mention that combined paint/hardener in the gun should be shaken or stirred periodically when using the satin

Tricks with MonoKote

LANDING-GEAR DOORS

Having introduced you to the usefulness of Super MonoKote as a release agent for polyester materials, I will now show you how to use it to help make doors.

1 On the wing's bottom sheeting, the areas where the landing-gear (LG) doors will go should be marked out and covered with MonoKote.

2 Brush a coat of resin over the MonoKote, and let it harden.

3 Lay up 2 or 3 layers of 10-ounce glass cloth coated with resin over the MonoKote.

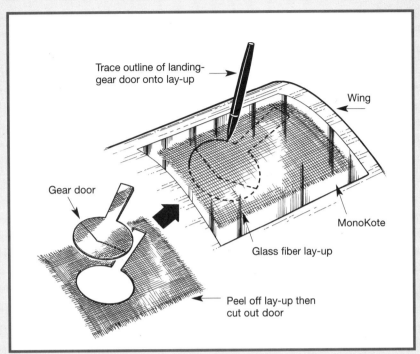

Retractable landing-gear doors are easy to make: use several layers of fiberglass cloth applied over a section of the wing that's protected by a MonoKote barrier.

4 When the resin has cured, sand the outer surface smooth. Prime it and re-sand.

5 Break away the fiberglass lay-up from the wing. Mark out the exact shape of the door, and cut it to size.

6 Remove the MonoKote, and lay the completed door on the wing (note that it follows every curve and twist and exactly fits the wing where it will be when it's retracted). Trace the door outline, and cut away the appropriate area of sheeting from the wing. Mount the door on the LG leg.

In addition to fitting precisely, LG doors made this way are strong and can't be bent out of shape.

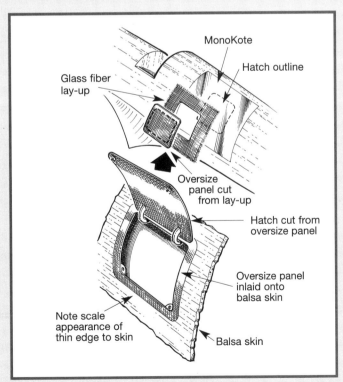

Details such as functional fuselage hatches can be made with fiberglass cloth applied over MonoKote.

hardener, or variations in sheen and drying times may be encountered.

So much for paints. There are a couple of other very useful products that we use extensively. One is microballoons. This is an ultralight powder filler which, when mixed with K&B resin, makes excellent fillets. It's handy for a number of other jobs, too, which I'll mention later. Of the many brands and two basic kinds available, I favor the brown "phenolic microballoons" made by Prather Products*. This company also makes a silica (pourable) version, but I've found this kind to be less desirable.

• **Metal or wood-covered aircraft.** To properly prepare you (forewarned is forearmed), I'll preface this section with a warning. Compared with finishing a fabric-covered aircraft, the achievement of

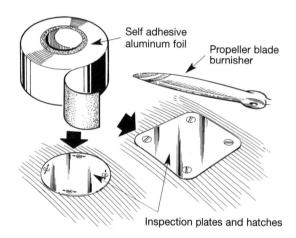

Self adhesive aluminum foil

Propeller blade burnisher

Inspection plates and hatches

Access hatches are easily duplicated with aluminum tape; cut it to shape, stick it into place, and burnish it smooth with a nylon propeller. To complete the detail, screw details are pressed onto the tape.

a grade-A finishing job on a metal subject requires infinitely more skill and more difficult techniques. Many additional features present themselves; among these are such typical surface details as panel lines, hatches and rivets. In particular, weathering techniques are much more complicated for a metal subject.

That's the bad news; now for the good. Whereas fabric-covered models oblige us to use some materials we'd prefer to avoid, we don't have this limitation on solid-surface subjects. We can use fiberglass covering and resin-finishing materials throughout. Then, too, the extra work shows, and these aircraft have a tendency to look prettier and possess more character. But, before we get into a detailed description of the fiberglass finishing

process, two very important areas need to be handled: fillets and landing-gear doors (see "MonoKote Tricks").

• **Fiberglass.** At first encounter, finishing a model with fiberglass and polyester resin sometimes proves to be a little messy. As you gain experience, the mess diminishes, and you'll enjoy the process more. Here's the procedure:

You'll need: glass cloth, K&B resin, hardener, a no. 12 artist's hog-hair brush, mixing cups and stirrers. Put some clean acetone into a jar (use it to clean the brush). Get scissors, a sanding block with 220-grit sandpaper and some paper towels or a roll of toilet paper.

Prepare the bare wooden parts with the usual fine sanding, spackle filling and re-sanding until they're really smooth.

Cut a piece of glass cloth to fit the section to be covered. No material takes compound curves as easily as glass, so you can cover a large section— half a fuselage, for instance—with one piece.

Mix the K&B resin 1 ounce at a time with eight drops of hardener. Brush the resin mixture onto the cloth. "Pull" the resin over as large an area as possible (make it go as far as you can). Work quickly.

When the 1 ounce of resin has been used, clean the brush and blot any "wet"-looking spots with the paper.

As the resin cures (about ½ hour), trim and feather the cloth's edges with the sanding block. Proceed with more covering, mixing 1 ounce of resin and eight drops of hardener at a time and cleaning the brush immediately after using each mixture.

Polyester resins have one slightly disturbing characteristic: they will not tolerate oils, and you'll get an uncured mess if you try to apply them over "oily" substances, which include epoxies, butyrate dope, greasy fingerprints, etc. All epoxy seams should be sealed with nitrate dope, Ambroid, or white glue and allowed to dry for 24 hours. Before applying the resin, use a rag dampened slightly with acetone to swab the fuselage. Also, if any "wet" spots appear after the first coat has been applied, sand these to remove the oily skin that characteristically forms as the resin cures. Wiping again with acetone prior to brushing on the second coat is prudent.

With the entire model covered, lightly sand and mix a big enough batch of resin to give an overall "flow-coat." When this has cured, sand carefully using 80- or even 60-grit aluminum-oxide sandpaper at first, and finish with 220-grit. The resin cuts the sandpaper as much as the sandpaper cuts the resin, so replace the sandpaper frequently. Note: we

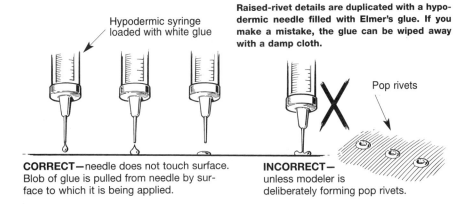

Hypodermic syringe loaded with white glue

Raised-rivet details are duplicated with a hypodermic needle filled with Elmer's glue. If you make a mistake, the glue can be wiped away with a damp cloth.

Pop rivets

CORRECT—needle does not touch surface. Blob of glue is pulled from needle by surface to which it is being applied.

INCORRECT— unless modeler is deliberately forming pop rivets.

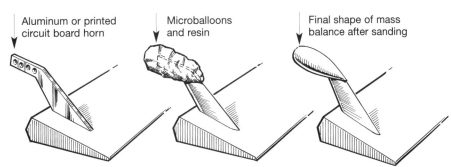

Aluminum or printed circuit board horn

Microballoons and resin

Final shape of mass balance after sanding

MASS BALANCE—example of detail fabricated from phenolic microballoons and resin.

Many details can be made with a mixture of phenolic microballoons and polyester resin. For an aileron mass balance, simply apply a blob of the mixture, and when it starts to gel, rough-shape it. When it has fully cured, sand it to final shape.

want to fill the weave of the cloth only. Sand away all excess resin until you can see the weave, but don't cut into the cloth. This is where many first-timers go wrong and get a heavy finish; they don't sand off enough resin.

Examine the results critically, re-apply resin, and sand out any bad areas.

• **Primer.** Now we can proceed to spray on the primer coat. When the primer has cured, sand lightly with 220-grit sandpaper. Because of the color of the primer, bad areas will usually show where we didn't notice them before. Treat all of these areas with more primer. Really deep dings or holes can be filled with acrylic auto-glazing putty. Sand lightly over all.

At this point, the model should look really great. Indeed, it needs to, because this is as good as it's going to get. However, the ship still looks bare, so let's add some details to it.

SURFACE DETAILS

• **Hatches.** Cut these to size out of aluminum air-conditioning tape. Peel off the paper backing to expose the adhesive, and smooth the tape down onto the

model, using a nylon prop as a burnishing tool. This material will follow compound curves to some degree, because it is only 0.003 inch thick and is soft-tempered.

• **Panel lines.** Mark the panel lines directly on the primed model with a soft pencil. Over these, lay 1/64-inch-wide chart tape (available at drafting and office-supply outlets). Use the flexible type (Formaline no. 5000A, or an equivalent), which is easy to form around sharp curves. This tape may be left on the model permanently, or (as I prefer) it can be removed after the model has been painted and prior to the final clearcoat. This method gives very realistic simulated panel joints.

• **Rivets.** Use Elmer's white glue, applying it with a hypodermic needle. The glue droplet will stick to the model and be pulled off the end of the needle. The needle must not touch the model, or the rivet will lose its roundness and assume a "fried egg" appearance. Thin the glue with water, if necessary, but go easy.

• **Other details.** Many small details, such as fairings for antenna masts, streamlined forms on aileron mass-balances, air scoops and blisters, can be made with microballoons. Put a blob of mixed microballoons and K&B resin into place, and simply carve it to shape and sand when it has cured. Small touches like this take a little extra effort, but they add much to the effectiveness of the finished model.

Now your model is ready for paint. Ah, but this is another story. Find my article on painting and weathering elsewhere in this book.

*Addresses are listed alphabetically in the Index of Manufacturers on page 146. +

Custom-mixing colors and weathering secrets

by Dave Platt

Editors' note: Dave says that the paint job on a scale model is the most enjoyable part of model building. We say it's fun when it's done well; here's how.

I need to begin by explaining why an oft-requested item is not available. Modelers frequently ask for "formulas" for certain colors (military shades, for instance). These fellows suppose that if they had a formula (so many parts white, so many blue and so on), they'd be able to match a color without difficulty. But such formulas are not available because they won't work. Minute shade variations in any ingredient will spoil everything—so will variations in strength (pigment-to-carrier relationship). No paint manufacturer will claim zero variation in either of these qualities.

Pat McCurrie's ⅕-scale Bf 109 G-6 scheme is a good example of the Luftwaffe's winter camouflage.

Here are a few basic mixing facts to show how these are incorporated to get the color you want:
- Red + yellow + blue = brown
- Yellow + blue = green
- Yellow + red = orange
- Blue + red = violet
- White + black = gray
- White lightens; black darkens.

LUFTWAFFE COLORS

Let's take an example and see how we'd make a specific color. Suppose I want to make RLM no. 75. This is a violet gray. Gray is white and black, so to this we add some blue and red. Proceed as follows: Start with half a can of white. Add a little blue and a good slug of red (Hobby Poxy* H-66 Red only). Try out samples. It takes a while to zero in on any color, even a simple one. Small dabs of

The Messerschmitt Bf-109 has a unique camouflage scheme, so it makes a good example for a discussion of mixing custom-paint colors.

Consequently, formulas won't work and, indeed, it would be a disservice to modelers to attempt such a project, because it would only be misleading.

CUSTOM-MIXING COLORS

Bearing this in mind, it's still often necessary to custom-mix a batch of paint for a model. Given a basic understanding of how colors work, this is not a particularly hard thing to do.

There are only three primary colors: red, yellow and blue. Any other color can be made using these. The primaries can't be made by mixing any colors. Black and white are not colors (they are tones), but we must consider them as essential in color-matching, because tone must be matched, too.

Nick Ziroli Jr.'s impressive Grumman F6F Hellcat has a lot of character. Painted markings, chipped paint and realistic wear marks on the wing and the fuselage sides just under the cockpit make it look like a well-used fighting machine.

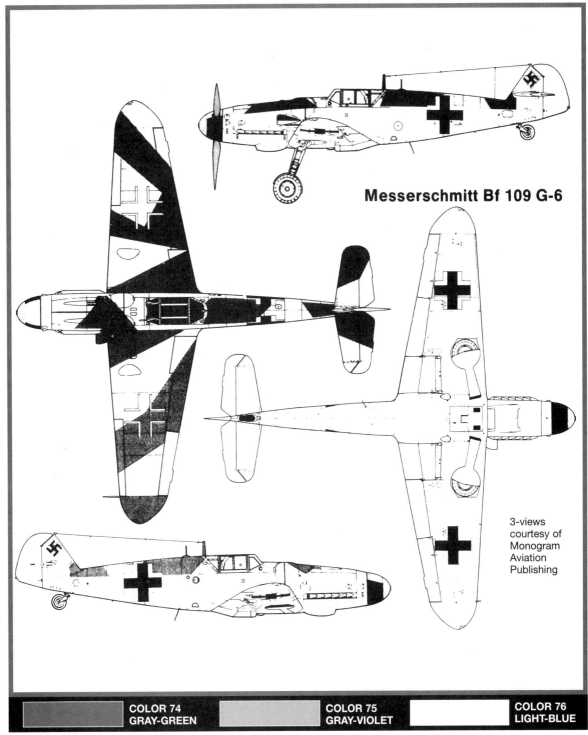

Messerschmitt Bf 109 G-6

3-views
courtesy of
Monogram
Aviation
Publishing

COLOR 74 GRAY-GREEN	COLOR 75 GRAY-VIOLET	COLOR 76 LIGHT-BLUE

When you paint your Messerschmitt 109, this scale drawing (from "The Official Monogram Painting Guide to German Aircraft, 1935-1945") is a good reference.

paint for correction will do, once an approximation has been obtained. The vital thing about learning to match colors is to get in there and start! No amount of hand-wringing gets the job done, but mixing paint will. At first, mix small amounts, and plan to spend an evening or two on learning this essential skill.

In some ways, this is a more difficult subject to describe than any other, because it is essentially a visual process. We'll give one more example, and leave it for practical experiment by the modeler.

To make RLM no. 76, start with white. Add black to get a pale gray. Add a little blue to get a pale blue-gray. This color has a faint greenish tinge;

Above: Bob Karlsson's Grumman F4F Wildcat has the classic exhaust stains on its fuselage side. Before you add such a detail, make sure it's characteristic of your subject aircraft. Right: dirt, grease and grime add character to the detail on Bob's Wildcat landing gear.

the colors to merge either. The correct effect is obtained by aiming for the "hardest" division possible with a spray gun. Spray the stab next, then the no. 75 areas of the fuselage spine and, finally, a light "mottle" on the sides among the no. 75 mottles already there. To get the idea of the shape and size of realistic mottling, copy a photograph of a full-size 109.

When the model has been painted to this point, lightly sand it with wet 600-grit paper, using plenty of water. This will remove the tiny "spikes" of dry paint and any powdery areas. Spray the wings and stabs in a chordwise direction and the fuselage up and down.

add a little yellow (which, when combined with the blue in the mix, will send the color in a green direction). So, no. 76 consists of four paints. Use only a lemon (blue) yellow; a chrome yellow will prevent a proper match because of the red that's inherent in the yellow.

PAINTING THE MODEL

Assuming that we have mixed the required colors and have a supply of every color needed for the model, let's proceed. I'll use the example of the Me 109 to show the order of procedures.

One basic tenet that holds true in any paint job is that lighter colors should be applied first. This being so, spray the underside and fuselage sides with no. 76. Next, apply no. 75 (the lighter of the two upper-surface colors) to the tops of the wings and the stabilizer. Also apply no. 75 along the upper "spine" of the fuselage. All divisions between the lower no. 76 and upper no. 75 should be fairly "hard" (but not masked) lines.

Now the fuselage sides are faintly mottled here and there with no. 75 over no. 76. Restrict the spray-gun delivery until a soft effect is obtained; we don't want "blobs." Spray the fin and rudder in a similar way. When no. 75 has been satisfactorily applied, proceed to the darker no. 74 upper color. Paint the wings first. Following the plans carefully, use a spray gun to "draw" the outlines of the no. 74 areas, then fill in between the lines with paint. Here again, although we don't want a firm line such as masking would give, we don't want

MARKINGS

There are basically two ways to apply markings:
• Paint
• Decals—the traditional "water-slide" variety and the vinyl or Mylar stick-on type.

This is, of course, purely an opinion, but I think that the stick-on decals are fine only on a ready-to-fly .049 U-control model. They have no place on a scale model; a vinyl decal will seriously mar the scale appearance, no matter how good the rest of the model may be.

The ordinary water-slide decal (a vanishing breed) is OK for most purposes and has the great virtue of being quick to apply. There are a couple of things to watch out for with decals:
• Sometimes, they are printed "out of register" (one of the colors is misplaced in relation to another). This can't usually be corrected; the sheet must be discarded.
• The final clearcoat may react with the decal, causing it to wrinkle, become crazed, or blistered. Assuming you don't have either of these problems, water-slide decals are fine. They need care in application.

Here are a few hints:
• Soak the decal briefly in water. It will probably curl up. Don't attempt to straighten it: you'll crack it. It will flatten out by itself as the water impregnates the paper more fully.
• Moisten the area of the model where the decal

will go. Slide the decal into place, and adjust its position.

• Using a piece of wetted soft balsa, squeegee out all trapped water. Sponge clean and then dry.

• Allow the decal to dry for at least 24 hours before you spray it with clearcoat.

One-Color Decals

One very good system is to use a one-color water-slide sheet of decal paper (I provide this in my kits). This has the great advantage of flexibility; you can cut out the markings you want for your chosen version and you won't have to settle for the identical markings that every other buyer of that kit received. A secondary benefit of this paper is that there is no clear carrier-coat to trim away.

Painted Markings

I've saved painted markings till last because this, I feel, is the best method of all. Certainly, it is the chosen method of the experts. There are two excellent reasons for suffering the extra work and time taken to paint the markings on. First, paint follows any shape and compound curve and goes over rivets, etc.; decals can be a nuisance here. Second, the markings can be weathered along with the rest of the model. You can't do that with decals! Liquid Masking Film, such as Bob Dively Model Aircraft's* product, will give you the cleanest, most precise markings possible. The directions included with this product are very comprehensive, and I can't do better than suggest you do it as the manufacturer tells you to. Perhaps the best recommendation I can give is to say that I use Liquid Masking Film on my own models. If you have stayed with this rather lengthy story this far, you'll be glad to know that relief is in sight! The most mysterious and baffling of all arts—weathering—is next.

Liquid Masking Film, such as this from Bob Dively Model Aircraft, produces the best results when you mask a model for scale markings.

BUILDING CHARACTER

All right; we've built it, covered it, sanded and sanded and sanded it. We've painted it and put the markings on. Sure looks like a finished model; it isn't! One vital ingredient is missing—one that controls a model's eventual effectiveness. This ingredient is "character." If we forget this, our nice models will always be just that—nice models and nothing more.

We must somehow capture the dignity of the full-size flying machine. Sound a bit romantic? Well, perhaps it is. But if we can at least be aware of this mysterious something that emanates from an airplane, we are on the road to creating a work of art that transcends the model and becomes a true replica. Let's discuss how we might inject this "character."

An airplane is a tool; it's a tool for doing a specific job. That job may be to carry passengers or its owner from point A to point B; in this case, it's a vehicle of transportation, like a car. Or its job could be to destroy: to drop bombs, shoot up or shoot down the enemy's tools. Because an airplane is a tool, it is subjected to the same treatment as any other tool: a whole lot of abuse and a whole "little of" respect. It's called upon to do its job (often, it does more than it was designed for) with unfailing willingness and reliability, coupled with the minimum of essential care and maintenance.

Let's itemize some of the effects that this "love and attention" have on the appearance of an airplane and, also, some other factors on an airplane that are not manmade. These are, in order of importance:

• Color perspective
• Use
• Mechanical
• Weather

Did you notice something unusual about this list? Adding realistic effects to a model is commonly known as "weathering." Yet, I'm asking you to believe that not only is weather just one of four major factors that affect airplanes, but it's also of the least import! How come? Let's take each item singly, and the answer will be revealed.

Color Perspective

Stand by a tree. You'll see that the bark is brown and the leaves are green, but there are many shades of each. Now move 100 yards away, and look again. Right away, the varied shades have disappeared, and the trunk is plain brown, while the leaves are an overall green.

Move another ¼ mile away, and you'll see a much more even color throughout; the brown seems less brown, and the green less green. As a matter of fact, it would be difficult to tell just what color a tree is at this distance, if we didn't already know from experience. Move even farther

Tools of the Trade

Apart from masking tape and the usual stuff found in any modeler's workshop, there is really only one other tool that you'll need. This is an airbrush—a really good one. The type that has a hole that you block with your finger to spray, then release to stop, is fine for plastic models, but it will not do for really intricate detail. You need an airbrush that has a trigger that's controlled by a screw, so that you can adjust the flow of paint. Get the right kind of airbrush, and it will serve you well.

Such airbrushes are not cheap; mine cost nearly $100 (without the compressor). The compressor should be fitted with a water trap, or you will be forever blowing out the water that forms when air is compressed. Usually, high humidity and/or small nozzle openings aggravate this problem.

There are a lot of airbrushes available for various tasks. For precise paint delivery, I use one with a trigger that can be adjusted with a screw.

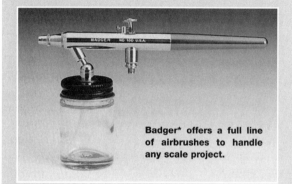

Badger* offers a full line of airbrushes to handle any scale project.

Whichever air compressor you use, avoid splattering water on your model on humid days by fitting the compressor with a water trap.

away; now the tree is on the horizon, 1½ miles away. It's now a medium gray all over with no discernible color distinctions.

This effect is known as "color perspective." It happens because the air we look through is neither as clean nor as transparent as we think it is. Between our eyes and the tree, there is airborne dust in untold quantities. That dust is gray, and it acts like a giant diffuser.

What difference does this make to our scale model? Consider this: looking at an ⅛-scale model from 10 feet is the same as looking at the real plane from 80 feet—right? Wrong! It's wrong because, when we look at the big one, there is eight times as much atmosphere between our eyes and the real plane as there is between our eyes and the model. To our eyes, this has the effect of toning down the colors on the real plane more than it tones down those on the model. We must compensate for this "visual scale distance." We do it by giving the model an even and very light spray-coat of medium-gray after the color

scheme has been completed and all the markings have been applied. The coat should cover all surfaces, including the glass areas.

Color perspective gets first place on the list because it's inevitable. Even a model of a so-called "factory-fresh," unused airplane is subject to this universal inevitability. Having mentioned "factory-fresh," let's explode another myth. Many times, a builder of a glass-smooth scale model will excuse himself by falling back on the old saw that his model represents a "factory-fresh" airplane. So how, one asks, did it get squadron markings and crest and a victory tally?

Use
Chronologically, the next changes in the appearance of a full-size plane are caused by use. We can subdivide these changes according to five major causes.
• Dirt and grime
• Paint chipping and scratches
• Oil and fuel stains
• Burns
• Damage

Dirt and grime are best represented by careful and very soft sprays of dark charcoal gray on the completed model. Remember that dirt normally follows line of flight. Thus, it will collect behind protuberances on the aircraft and diminish as the distance from the protuberance increases. Panels of slightly unequal levels, e.g., along wing, stab and fuselage sheeting joints, especially those that are perpendicular to the line of flight, also show the effect to a lesser extent.

Paint chipping and scratches. Simulate this with silver paint on a small, stiff-hair brush that has been scrubbed on a piece of scrap paper until it's almost dry. Jab the brush onto the model to leave irregularly shaped wear marks. These marks most commonly occur at the places where the crew enters the plane and where mechanics perform routine work. Fuel fillers, ammunition bays and inspection hatches gather wear of this kind in an unbelievably short time, especially during military use, where a proud owner is not around to moan about the small dings! Keep the silver where it belongs. We don't want the model to look like some full-size plane that got left out in a sandstorm.

Oil and fuel stains are best applied by rubbing the model at the appropriate places with some staining agent and soft cheesecloth. Use nearly black or fawn to simulate burns around the exhaust pipe and soot from the exhaust on a full-size craft. You might want to browse in the model railroad department at the hobby shop for colors that are used to weather trains.

Burns. Before applying exhaust burns, find out whether marks of this kind are characteristics of your type of plane. Skyraiders always have these marks; Spitfires seldom do. This brings up an important point: study as many photos as possible of your subject. Look "through" the jazzy schemes and study the "use" marks, noting which ones seem to occur consistently. Concentrate on these.

Damage, of course, can happen anywhere at any time and to any degree. This is impossible to detail. Just use your imagination. But go easy!

Mechanical. The mechanical causes of significant appearance changes are repairs and holes. Repairs to an aircraft typically take the form of patches on damaged metal or fabric. Very often, patches on metal structures have fresh paint that shows as a sharply contrasting shade, even when the colors are the same. Fabric patches may have the same treatment, or they can be painted in red primary dope, which often is left just this way. In wartime, it was not uncommon to encounter airplanes with dozens of red patches. Imagine the situation: someone decides to add some device or another to an airplane, and he goes ahead and bolts it into place. Later, it's decided to remove the gadget. Do you think that anyone would bother to fill in the holes after removing it? No way! Here again, use your imagination, but once more, don't overdo it.

Weathering. So, finally, we come to weathering. I say "finally," because the other things described rapidly affect the appearance of an airplane, whereas weathering takes time. Even then, the effects are subtle, and a good deal of caution is necessary here. The visible effects of weathering are fading, cracking, peeling, rust and other corrosion. All paints fade in time. Under certain conditions, such as continued exposure to strong sunlight, noticeable fading can happen in two months.

Fading can be simulated by spraying a very light coat of pale gray from a distance and merging irregular formations. The upper surfaces of the wings and stab and the top of the fuselage fade more rapidly than the sides of the fuselage and the fin, and the entire undersurface scarcely changes at all. Cracking and peeling are best simulated by flaking off the occasional area of paint with a knife.

Here's another trick: after spraying on the color, before it has a chance to cure properly and become fuelproof, put some fuel on a rag and rub it onto a section of the plane. The paint will lift and flake off.

Rust is easy. Simply buy a bottle of rust enamel paint from a hobby shop (sold for model railroad use), and paint it on. Don't use too much; airplanes may be tatty and beaten, but rusty they aren't. The odd spot here and there is all you need.

So go ahead and try your hand at scale painting. As with any new experience, mistakes will be made, and your first results may be far from good, but persistence will eventually be rewarded.

Addresses are listed alphabetically in the Index of Manufacturers on page 146. ⬥

Cover a model with Stits Lite

by Gerry Yarrish

There are perhaps as many ways to duplicate a scale cloth finish as there are types of models. I've tried many techniques, all of which have good and bad points. The Stits Lite process from F&M Enterprises* is one of the easiest painting systems I've tried. Since Stits Lite uses the covering and finishing materials that are used on full-size aircraft (specially formulated and packaged for models), there's no question that the results are scale.

The basic ingredients are the heat-shrinkable Stits Lite polyester covering cloth, Poly-Tak fabric adhesive, Poly-Brush cloth sealant/primer, Poly-Spray silver pigmented undercoat and Poly-Tone color coat. All the materials used in the Stits Lite process are one-part, air-dry compounds that dry very quickly. Each part was formulated to work perfectly with the others, and F&M Enterprises does not recommend any substitutions of adhesives or paints, nor does it guarantee satisfactory results with any other polyester-cloth-covering materials. Here's how it's done:

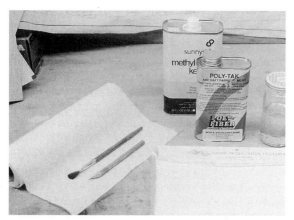

1 The few items you need to get started are Stits Lite covering, Poly-Tak adhesive, a ½- to ¾-inch-wide brush, a sharp hobby knife, paper towels and methyl ethyl ketone (MEK), which is used for cleanup.

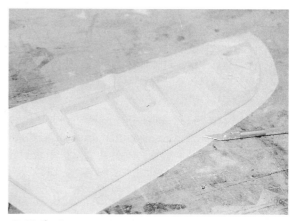

3 Place the part to be covered over the cloth, and with a sharp hobby knife, cut the cloth slightly oversize (about ½ inch larger all around).

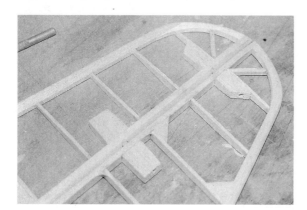

2 Here are the stab and elevator for my Aeroplane Works* PT-17 ready to cover. For a good finish, sand the model smooth, and fill all the dings, dents and pinholes with a good, easy-to-sand filler. I used Carl Goldberg's* Model Magic filler. Note the balsa blocks added for proper hinge support.

4 Brush on a coat of Poly-Tak adhesive. I find it easier to first pour the adhesive into a wide-mouth glass container than to use it straight from the metal can it comes in. Apply the adhesive quickly, and put the cloth into place while the adhesive is still wet.

5 Work the cloth into the adhesive with your fingers for a good bond with all the contact points.

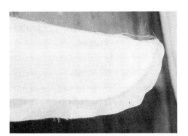

6 Pull the cloth down all around the perimeter, and pull it lengthwise to remove any large creases or wrinkles.

7 Trim the edges of the cloth to about a ¼-inch width, apply Poly-Tak to the cloth's underside and attach it to all the edges.

8 Here's the covered elevator. Note that there are no wrinkles even though the cloth has not been heat-shrunk. Now repeat the process on the part's uncovered side. Only after the part has been completely covered and all the edges have been glued down should you apply heat to tighten the covering. When you heat the cloth, use a covering iron, not a heat gun. A heat gun can overheat the cloth and damage it. Initially, set the temperature at about 250 degrees F. For the final tightening, use about 325 degrees F.

9 Here, the covered horizontal stab and elevators have been fitted to the fuselage so that the vertical stab can be glued into place before the rest of the fuselage is covered. Note that the fairing block under the vertical stab was covered with cloth before the vertical stab was added. The cloth was cut away at the contact point for the vertical stab before the stab was glued into place.

10 Start to cover the fuselage on the bottom. First, brush the glue onto the structure, and then apply the cloth while the glue is still wet. Here, I am pressing the cloth down with the brush at the trailing edge of the wing saddle. For a smooth bond, you can also apply MEK over the bonded area with the brush. The solvent seeps through the cloth and activates the adhesive beneath.

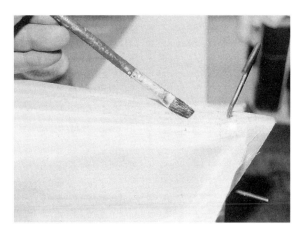

11 Pull the cloth taut toward the tail, and tack it down with more glue. Next, working around the edges, pull the cloth taut, and tack it into place with more adhesive on the stringers.

12 When the glue is dry, trim the cloth at the stringers as shown here. Again, note that all wrinkles have been removed before the cloth is heat-shrunk.

13 Next, apply cloth to the side of the fuselage, starting at the top "corner" stringer of the fuselage and going to the edge of the covered bottom. When you trim the edges, place a piece of cardboard under the side covering. This way, you can produce a clean, straight edge without cutting into the underlying cloth. Repeat the process for the other fuselage side, then cover the top of the fuselage (turtle deck).

14 Once all the surfaces of the fuselage and tail parts have been covered and heat-shrunk, brush on a coat of Poly-Brush cloth sealant/primer. Poly-Brush dries very quickly, so apply it to small sections at a time, and avoid brushing over areas already coated. To strengthen and improve the appearance of the overlapping seams, apply ½-inch-wide Stits Lite pinked tape evenly over the seams. First, apply a coat of Poly-Brush over the seam, and press the tape down into the wet Poly-Brush. Apply another coat of Poly-Brush over the tape, and stipple the material into the tape so that there are no bubbles or voids under it.

15 Here is a finished seam with pinked tape applied over it. After the Poly-Brush has dried (20 to 30 minutes), if there are any raised edges, you can run an iron (225 degrees F.) over the edges to seal the tape. This will greatly reduce the amount of sanding you have to do later on.

16 For the wing, apply Poly-Tak around the perimeter, and apply the bottom covering first. Wrap the edges of the cloth around the leading edge, tip and trailing edge, and work it down smooth with your fingers. Then apply the top covering, and again apply Poly-Tak along the underside of the edges, and press the cloth down for a smooth finish. Only after both the top and bottom surfaces have been covered and sealed around the edges should you heat-shrink the cloth.

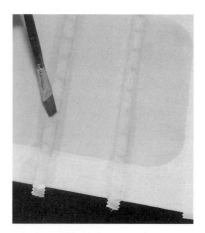

17 Once the cloth has tightened, brush on a coat of Poly-Brush, and let it dry. Work in small sections until the entire wing has been sealed. Now, if you want to add rib stitching and tape detail, add it before you apply the pinked tape around the wing's perimeter. Press all the edges of the tape down with a covering iron as mentioned earlier. When all the parts of your model have been covered and sealed, apply another coat of

Poly-Brush. If you wish, a third and final coat of Poly-Brush can be sprayed on, but I applied only two brushed coats. If you spray on the Poly-Brush, use about 40psi air pressure, and thin the Poly-Brush with Stits Lite Reducer (three parts Poly-Brush to one part Reducer). Allow about an hour to dry.

18 Wipe down the parts with a tack cloth, and spray on a coat of Poly-Spray (I use an automotive touch-up spray gun). When the first coat is dry, go over all the parts with 320-grit sandpaper, and remove any specks of dust or rough spots. Use a very light touch because it is easy to cut into the cloth that has sharp edges beneath. Poly-Spray has an aluminum pigment (silver in color) that gives the cloth opacity and a uniform undercoat for the final color coat. Wipe it down with a tack cloth again, and spray on a second coat. Apply this coat "wet" so that the material will flow evenly. If the Poly-Brush dries too quickly, add about 30 percent Reducer to slow the drying process. Now set aside and let dry for a day or two.

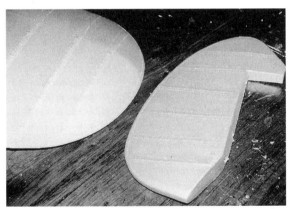

19 Spray on two coats of Poly-Tone color coat, and let dry. Poly-Tone has a lot of pigment, covers very well and comes out of the can ready to shoot through your gun. Reducer has already been added, as have blush retarder (for humid conditions) and "fish-eye" eliminator (for small imperfections in the finish caused by surface impurities). Before you apply any masking tape for trim painting, allow a couple of hours to dry, and you've finished.

As you can see, there are a number of steps in covering a model with Stits Lite, but it all boils down to: (1) covering the model, (2) applying a sealant/primer, (3) spraying on a silver undercoat and (4) spraying the final color coat. That's it; it's simple and looks great. Best of all, you use the same materials as those used on full-size aircraft. You can't get any more scale than that.

Addresses are listed alphabetically in the Index of Manufacturers on page 146. ✦

Make scale rib stitching

by Gerry Yarrish

You never know just where a good building or finishing technique will pop up. At this year's Top Gun Scale Invitational, I "talked scale" with modeling friend Cliff Tacie; I commented that the rib stitching on his Fly Baby looked really great. At the time, I was trying to figure out a quick and easy way to duplicate this detail on my Ziroli/Aeroplane Works* Stearman PT-17 shown here. In about 10 minutes, Cliff explained his technique; and you know what? It's the easiest I've tried. Naturally, I stole it! Here it is (with a few modifications). Cliff gets all the credit!

The method is best for ⅕-scale models and larger ones.

MATERIALS

- ½ inch-wide pinked finishing tape—F&M Enterprises*
- Fabric sealant/primer—F&M Poly-Brush—or nitrate dope
- Poly-Tak adhesive—F&M
- Balsarite adhesive—Coverite*
- Solvent—MEK (methyl ethyl ketone)
- Flat piece of plywood
- Graph paper
- Brads
- Spool of cotton thread
- Brush
- Scissors
- Hobby knife
- Straightedge
- Small hammer
- Covering iron—Coverite
- Heat gun

1 Coat the graph paper with two coats of Balsarite, and let it dry.

2 Position the graph paper over the plywood, and hammer the small brads along one edge of it at the spacing that you want your rib stitching to be. (For a ⅕-scale model, 1-inch spaces represent a 5-inch, full-scale, rib-stitch spacing. I decided on ½-inch spacing for the tail-feather stitching.)

3 Do the same along the other side of the graph paper. Notice that the brads are angled outward slightly.

4 Starting at the top left corner, wrap the cotton thread back and forth around the brads as shown here. The brads' outward cant makes the thread lie flat against the paper.

5 Apply a thick coat of Balsarite over the thread to bond it to the paper. Use a lot of it; if you don't, the thread may lift off the paper later.

6 Place a couple of scrap-balsa sticks under the paper as shown. When the paper is wetted with Balsarite, it tends to expand a little, and the string doesn't lie flat. The sticks raise the paper slightly so that it becomes taut and allows the thread to bond completely to it.

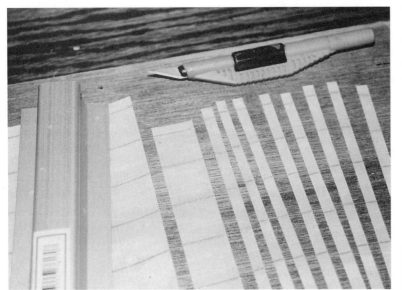

7 When the Balsarite has dried completely, remove the brads and cut the paper into strips with a straightedge and a hobby knife. The graph paper makes it very easy to cut straight strips. Here, I've cut ³⁄₁₆-inch-wide strips to match the width of my wing's capstrips.

8 These ³⁄₃₂-inch-wide strips are for the rudder, elevators and horizontal stab. If, when you cut the paper, some of the threads pull away from it, carefully reposition them and dab them with a little MEK. This will reactivate the Balsarite and re-glue the threads into place.

9 Prime your model's cloth covering with one coat of Poly-Brush (or nitrate dope, depending on your finishing process), then apply a second coat—a thick one—along the top of the rib.

10 Place the rib-stitching over the rib, and dab it into place with the brush. Then apply a second coat—a flow coat—over it, and go on to the next rib. As you apply the strips, try to keep the "stitches" in line with one another. I use the edge of the control surface or wing as a guide. Also, it is quicker to cut all the strips to length before you start to glue them into place.

11 When all the strips are in place, cut all the pinked surface tapes to length, and lay them over the ribs. Apply another coat of Poly-Brush over the stitches and, while stretching the tape slightly, apply it to the stitches, making sure it's centered on them and that about 1 inch of tape overhangs at either end. Do not wrap the tape around the edges. Continue this procedure until all the ribs have been covered.

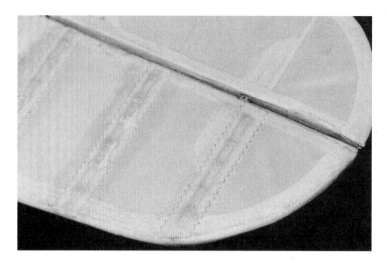

12 When the tapes are dry, cut off the overhangs with a sharp knife. Because you didn't wrap the tapes all the way around the edges, the tape around the perimeter will lie down more smoothly and look better. The perimeter tape is a little difficult to apply properly using only Poly-Brush. A better way is to cut the tape to length, and then apply Balsarite or Poly-Tak adhesive to its underside. While the adhesive is still wet, apply the tape to the leading edge and around the tip, stretching it slightly as you go. This means you have to work about 1 foot at a time and apply fresh adhesive as it's required. Don't try to smooth the entire tape down all at once; just make sure it's bonded into place along its center.

13 Next, with your covering iron set at about 225 degrees F., iron the tapes into place, working slowly along their length. I apply some MEK with a brush and smooth the tape into place with my fingers. Finally, coat the tape with Poly-Brush (or dope) as you did before. With all the rib stitching and pinked tape applied and sealed into place, the model is ready for paint.

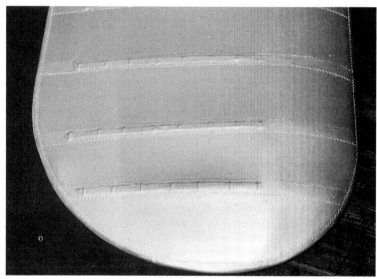

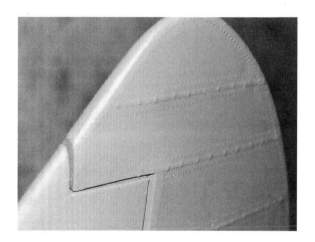

For models smaller than ⅕ scale, here's a little secret that F&M's Chip Mull shared with me: before you apply it to your model, shrink the pinked tape by heating it with your iron; ½-inch tape shrinks to about ⅜ inch.

For competition scale models, here's a hint. Full-size aircraft have wing ribs made of formed sheet metal or built up with spruce strips, and they're about ¼ to ⅝ inch wide. The ¼- or 3⁄16-inch capstrips commonly used on most sport models are too wide for an accurate scale appearance. Use rib capstrips that are the same width as or slightly wider than the rib itself (3⁄32 to ⅛ inch).

Addresses are listed alphabetically in the Index of Manufacturers on page 146.

Repair Stits Lite cloth

by Gerry Yarrish

OK, how would you react to this statement? "Uh, Gerry, I uh, just stepped on your wing, and it sounded really bad!" My first reaction was to tell my flying buddy to knock it off; I don't like bad jokes. Imagine my surprise when I found out it *wasn't* a joke!

Accidents happen all the time, and you can either make the best of it or jump up and down and invent

new adjectives to describe your new-found "wing walker." I made the best of it; I wrote this "how-to" article to help others who might find themselves in a similar situation. Mind you, these repairs are not limited to damage inflicted by size 11 Reeboks or Nikes.

If you're far from home, make the necessary field repairs so you can salvage any remaining flight opportunities. If you're at home, just pack it in and head to the shop where you have all your tools. Now, let's fix that wing.

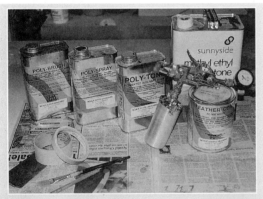

Repairing Stits Lite is an easy task. You'll need MEK solvent, Poly-Brush primer, Poly-Spray silver coat and Poly-Tone paint to match your old finish, sandpaper, masking tape, scissors, a sharp hobby knife and some sable hair brushes.

Keep some MEK solvent in a glass jar so you can keep your brush clean and ready to use. After each use, place the brush in the MEK. This will keep the adhesive from clumping and building up on the bristles.

1 At the field, remove the covering above the damaged ribs (cut neatly and save the covering material) and extend the opening one rib bay on either side of the repair site. Save all the small pieces rattling around inside the wing and clean out the wing as best as you can. Piece together the damaged ribs and glue everything with CA and kicker. (I used Pacer* thin and thick Zap for this). Add sheet balsa to either side of the damaged ribs and glue together.

If the spar or D-tube sheeting is also damaged, be sure to reinforce the damaged area properly. Sand smooth and then place the old covering back into place. Use a vinyl masking tape (clear, in this case) to hold the cloth in place. Use plenty of tape and, if necessary, apply some thin Zap around the edges to hold the cloth securely in place. This temporary patch job will save your weekend, but you should properly repair your wing as soon as possible.

2 Back in the shop, remove your field repair and take another look at your internal repairs. If you need to do some more work, now is the time to get it done. I have been using F&M Enterprises* Stits Lite fabric and paint for a while now, and I can tell you that this stuff is extremely easy to work with and repair.

While wearing latex rubber gloves, soak some paper towels with M.E.K. solvent and start wiping down the covering about an inch or two past your repair opening. Replace the MEK-soaked paper towels often, and slowly remove all of the old finish. The MEK will remove all the previous coats of paint to

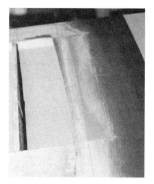

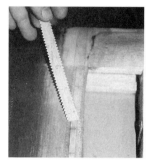

expose the raw Scale Stits cloth underneath. If you have surface details such as rib stitching, these too can be removed easily with MEK. When you have finished, you should have clean, raw cloth to which your repair patch may be attached.

3 To allow the patch cloth to lie flat on the wing, the edges of the old cloth that will be under the patch need to be feathered into the surface of the underlying balsa. F&M Feather Coat filler works well for this. Apply a thin layer of the filler around the perimeter of the repair area and let dry. Sand flat with 320-grit sandpaper, and reapply the filler as often as needed to bring the surface of the exposed structure up to that of the old cloth.

Do not overlook this step, as this would leave an unsightly ridge around the edges of the repair. Once the area has been sanded smooth, clean the area with a tack cloth to remove any dust.

4 Apply two coats of Poly-Tak adhesive to the repair area. Apply the adhesive to the balsa sheeting, the rib capstrips and to the cloth where the patch seam will be located. Also, apply a coat of the adhesive under the old cloth where it contacts the ribs and balsa sheeting.

5 Cut some new Stits Lite cloth to cover the repair area and make it about an inch larger than needed all around. Cover the repair area with the cloth and mark the cloth where it will need to be cut to fit properly into place. Place the edges of the patch over the ribs on either side of the repair area; you'll want these edges to be as straight as possible.

To prevent the cloth from fraying when it's cut, apply a coat of Poly-Brush primer to the cloth using your marks as a guide. Allow the primer to dry and then cut the patch cloth with a sharp pair of scissors.

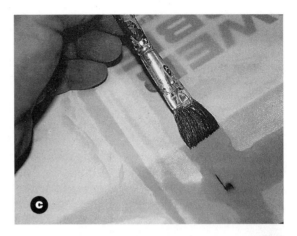

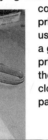

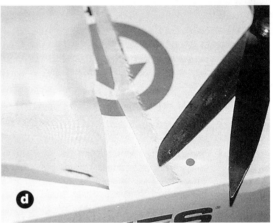

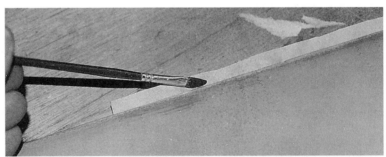

6 Put the cloth into place and position it so that the edges overlap with the ribs on either side of the repair. To attach the patch, brush on some MEK with a ½-inch-wide sable brush and allow the solvent to soak through the cloth. The MEK will activate the underlying Poly-Tak adhesive and will make the patch adhere. Pull the edges of the patch to remove any large wrinkles, but don't sweat any of the smaller ones. You will also need to apply adhesive to any edge that contacts the old finis, such as at the underside of the leading and trailing edges.

Allow 30 minutes for the adhesive to set and then shrink out any remaining wrinkles using an iron set at about 250 degrees F. Stits Lite shrinks up to 15 percent when heated, so apply the heat evenly to the entire patch until it has shrunk tight. Don't allow the iron to contact the old painted finish, as this may cause heat damage.

7 Apply two coats of Poly-Brush primer to the patch and let dry. Apply a final "flow" coat of the primer to the patch as well as to the surrounding cloth to blend the patch into the old finish. If you had surface details, now is the time to reapply them.

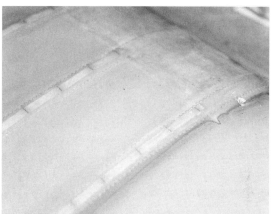

8 Here's what the new patch looks like after the Poly-Brush primer has been applied, and the surface details have been added. Note that the primer has been applied over the old finish about an inch all around. Now lightly scuff the patch with a Scotch Brite pad to remove any dried-on dust and then wipe the entire wing panel with a tack cloth to make sure the surface is completely free of dust.

9 Using an airbrush, apply three light coats of Poly-Spray to the patch. Feather the silver coat over the old finish about 3 inches all around and allow to dry between coats. Apply each coat at a 90-degree angle to the previous coat. I like to apply the Poly-Spray and the final coats of Poly-Tone paint while the wing is standing up on a wingtip. This allows the paint to be applied in a horizontal spray direction, and it also prevents any drips from falling onto the finished wing.

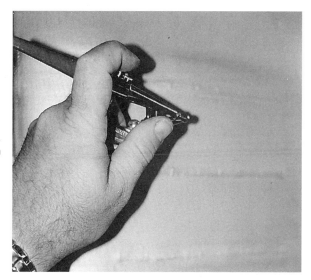

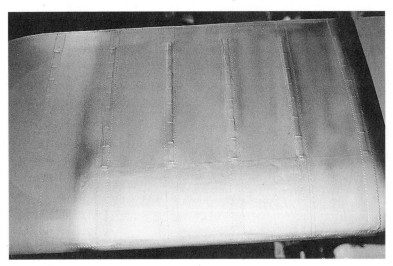

10 Once the Poly-Spray has dried (about 20 minutes), the patch is ready for the final two or three coats of Poly-Tone paint. Allow the Poly-Tone to dry for a day or two before you apply any decals, and you're done.

11 With a new decal applied to the wingtip, the damaged Stearman is again ready to fly.

Once you've finished the repair, only you will know that any damage was done to your plane. With Stits Lite, repairs can be invisible.

Addresses are listed alphabetically in the Index of Manufacturers on page 146. ✦

2

Dressing up your model

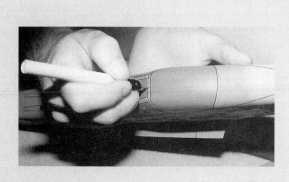

Use computer-generated details

by Randy Randoph

Almost everyone has access to a computer, and just about every computer has the software to generate large letters and numbers in many different styles. These photos show a simple way to use computer-generated characters with iron-on plastic films that will add detail to any project.

1 You'll need: a razor knife, plastic film, a steel straight-edge, a glue stick and computer-generated characters. These letters were done on a laser printer, but any printer will produce similar results.

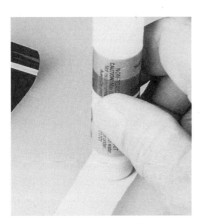

2 Coat the back of the character sheet with glue; be sure to spread glue over the entire back of the letters, all the way out to the edges. Stick the letters face up on the top side of the plastic film.

3 Use a metal straightedge and a razor knife to cut out the characters. To make the job a lot easier, place a cutting board or a piece of card stock under the film. Remove any plastic backing from the film characters.

4 Tack the characters, paper and all, where you want them to go on the airplane. (A trim iron is best, but any iron will do.) Laser-printed letters are heat-sensitive, and the iron will smudge them, so keep the iron in the center of the numbers when you tack them into place.

5 When the characters have been tacked into place, spray them with water to loosen the glue that holds the paper to the plastic film.

6 Wait a second or two, and then peel the paper away from the film. Flush the film with more water to remove any remaining glue, then wipe the water off. To remove air bubbles, use a soft cloth to smooth over the film characters before you permanently iron them down. ✦

PHOTOS BY RANDY RANDOLPH

Duplicate scale aircraft markings

by Gerry Yarrish

The saying "Beauty is only skin deep" holds true in scale modeling. To static judges, an average-built model that has a superior paint job and finish is more desirable than a perfectly built model that has a poor finish. It's what's up front that counts.

Making the job of duplicating scale aircraft markings and lettering easier for the scale modeler is a company called Aeroloft*. This article shows you how they do it and how easy it will be to achieve beautiful scale markings on your next model.

PHOTOS BY GERRY YARRISH

A scale model is only as good as its finish and markings. Duplicating scale-aircraft markings is easy with Aeroloft Design's dry transfers.

The full-size SNJ Texan that I used as my subject was once the lead aircraft for the Six of Diamonds aerobatic show team. After a few letters and phone calls, its owner, Dr. Joe Scognia, allowed me to examine the aircraft in minute detail.

One of the largest markings is the Star and Bars insignia, and even this is easy to apply. The wing and the fuselage insignias are the same size.

DOCUMENTATION

Unless yours is a sport-scale model—for which you can use off-the-shelf markings—you'll have to do some homework. Having the full-size aircraft available for measurements and photographs is the best situation. But even then, you'll need to keep track of your work to achieve accurate duplication in model form. You must know your subject in detail if you want a truly scale model when you've finished.

DOIN' IT RIGHT

Go to an airport, a museum, or an air show to find your subject aircraft. Find out who owns it, and write or call for permission to photograph it at the owner's convenience. Some owners are more than happy to help out, and you'll gain the most information from the person who knows the aircraft best (and, possibly, make a new friend). Be aware, though, that some owners are not interested in helping a stranger who is asking questions about their plane. If this is the case, pick another aircraft to model.

Take along a notebook, a sketch pad, copies of 3-view drawings of the subject aircraft and a good camera with lots of film. I use a Nikon 5005 with two lenses—a 70 to 210mm zoom and a 28 to 85mm lens. Agfa 35mm 100 ASA color-print film works well, and I always wait for a super-bright sunlit day to photograph. I also vary the exposure

Top: on the wing, "070" and "Jacksonville" again dominate. During the late '40s and early '50s, to discourage pilots from buzzing public areas, the military required that planes have unmistakable aircraft identification markings.
Above: go Navy! The Aeroloft markings are so thin that even fine panel lines show right through. Rivet details and hatch lines readily show where the markings have been applied.

and shutter-speed settings to ensure that at least some prints will be good enough to use in my documentation package.

PLAN OF ATTACK

Start with basic overall views of the full-size plane, and photograph its left, right, front and rear. Then take quarter shots such as ¼ front, ¾ rear left and right, etc.

Next, move closer and photograph all large insignias, nose numbers, squadron markings, etc. Try to photograph these straight on to minimize distortion, and avoid using full flash. Continue to move closer to the aircraft, and photograph all the markings—from tail numbers to nomenclature markings such as "Step Here," "No Step," "Handhold," etc. If you're replicating a military aircraft, you'll be amazed at how much lettering there is on the plane.

MEASUREMENTS

Photos alone are not enough to ensure the accurate execution of your model's finish. The next, and most important, step is to accurately measure the size and position of every stencil, marking and number you see, and record the figures so that you'll be able to refer to them back at the shop. This is also a requirement for having your markings duplicated and manufactured by Aeroloft Design; your markings will only be as accurate as the information you give to Aeroloft.

STANDARD FIGURES

Almost every U.S. military aircraft will be painted and marked according to military tech orders, and only aircraft and unit markings will vary. For example, all let-

Above: the author and his crew chief, 'Becca (right), show off the ⅕-scale Texan. Would there be any question as to where this Texan was based if it were to fly overhead? The green, highly visible fuselage and wing stripes identify it as an instrument-training aircraft.

Right: my model is unusual in that it has the aircraft's base name, rather than the usual A/C number, on its tail. This, as well as all the other markings, is done in military-block style.

Most visible are the nose numbers (the last three digits of the aircraft registration number). In cases where the marking has to be formed over a sharp edge (the 0 to the left), you can cut the marking at the break line to prevent it from wrinkling.

ters and numbers, regardless of size, will be in military-block style. The small nomenclature markings are usually applied with stencils and vary only in size. Nose art and personal insignias are the only non-standardized markings on the aircraft.

Start with the largest markings—i.e., Star and Bars insignias—and work your way down to the smallest "Ground Here" stencil. To make the process simpler, measure only the length of the insignia (bar end to bar end) and only the height of the letters. Write down all the measurements for the markings, and group the information according to style, size and color.

Document the positions of all these markings in your notebook using a common reference point; i.e., do not measure from marking to marking; rather, measure all marking positions from a fixed point on the airframe, such as the aft edge of the engine cowl or the rudder's hinge line. Record these measurements on sketches or on copies of your 3-view drawings. Make large blow-up sketches of the really detailed areas (small measurements) so that, when you've finished, you won't have to go back and re-measure.

Now, let's head to the shop. Don't forget to take your empty film boxes and thank the aircraft's owner for his help.

GETTING MARKED

Back in your shop, organize your photos, sketches and measurements, and specify which colors are required for the various markings (usually black,

Photos of a full-scale subject

The markings on the full-size SNJ. From fuel grade, to the pilot's name, to where it's safe to walk, a military aircraft is covered with warnings and identifications. Reproduced for your model, these markings turn a great model into a truly scale reproduction. Aeroloft makes it easier than you think. Those who wish to get photo documentation of my Jacksonville "070" SNJ should call Bob Banka's Scale Model Research*.

Here, an Aeroloft marking is being rubbed into place. Tape it into position and then start to burnish it at the center and work out to the edges.

insignia white, blue and red and international yellow). Include your model's scale size, and send your package off to Aeroloft.

Aeroloft's graphics are the thinnest I've ever used, and they're made exactly to order. They're so thin because they're manufactured with alcohol-based inks rather than paint. Aeroloft duplicates all their markings in a process that involves separate color plates (negatives shot with a camera) for each color of the original artwork. Ultraviolet light is then used to set each separated color before the next color is applied. All the work is done by hand, and the quality and durability of the markings are excellent.

You receive the markings on a carrier sheet, and they're protected with a cover sheet so they're very easy to store, position and apply. The markings may be transferred very easily if the room temperature is at or above 70 degrees Fahrenheit. At lower tem-

The closer you get, the more you see. Here's a good example of the stenciled markings that are common on military aircraft.

peratures, the adhesive will have to be pressed down a little harder for it to be released. I've used markings after storing them for six months and had no problems. Steve Slachta of Aeroloft recommends that you apply them as soon as possible, but if you do store them, keep them upright (they come in a slim cardboard box) and in a cool area.

APPLICATION

Before you apply the markings, you should have a smooth, beautifully applied finish on your model. I spray on Hobby Poxy* two-part paints with an automotive-quality air gun. This very durable paint is easy to apply, and it makes a perfect surface for dry-transfer markings.

Start by measuring and marking the positions for your markings (draw a light pencil line or mark). Cut each marking out of its parent carrier sheet so that it will be easier to manage, and then position it on your model. When you're satisfied that it's positioned correctly, tape it down, then lift one side (keeping the other side taped in position), remove the backing paper, and press the marking into place. Slowly and carefully burnish the marking (I use a plastic propeller), working from the center toward the edges. You'll see that the color of the marking has changed when it has been properly transferred to the model. Once you get the hang of it, this goes very quickly.

CLEARING OUT

Once they've been applied, the markings need a protective clear coat to seal them (they aren't fuel- or dope-proof) and to prevent scuff damage. Aeroloft recommends PPG Ditzler's automotive clear (available from most auto-paint suppliers). This paint dries as smooth as glass, and the finished model looks wonderful. Flattening agent can be added to the clear coat to obtain the desired degree of sheen or flatness. Let your model dry in a dust-free area for a couple of days, and avoid the temptation to test the finish with your fingers.

That's it; from documentation to markings application, the process is easy if you organize your work. Best of all, if you ever decide to build another model with the same markings, a phone call to Aeroloft will have another set of markings off to you in short order. All their markings are stored in a computer and can be duplicated quickly—even in different scale sizes. Aeroloft also offers many "generic" marking sheets including common lettering, stencils, rivets, panels and panel lines. Try Aeroloft markings for your next project; you'll love the results.

*Addresses are listed alphabetically in the Index of Manufacturers on page 146.

Make custom color decals

by Jim Sandquist

All too often, we find an airplane that we want to replicate, but then discover that decals aren't readily available. We could have decals custom-made by one of the commercial sources, but this can sometimes cost more than we want to spend.

With the color copiers now available in many offices, you can make good-quality decals for your aircraft quickly and easily. Color copiers use a very thin, coated paper that works very well as a decal when applied directly to a model. A clear coat is all that's required to protect it from fuel.

Top: me and my completed P-47. The decals were applied to the model's MonoKote-covered surface and then covered with clear MonoKote to protect and fuelproof them. Above: what do you do when you need special color decals for a particular model? You can have them commercially produced, but if you want to save a few bucks, you can make the decals yourself with an office color copier! Left: "seal coated" and applied to the airframe, the decal looks great. The words "Stearman Squadron" were hand-painted before the Baron Pizza logo was applied.

The process is quite simple:

• Get a photograph of the logo or artwork you want to duplicate as a decal for your model. It will help greatly if the original photo is larger than the size of the decal you want to apply to your plane. When the color copier reduces the original, the definition of the final decal will be greatly enhanced.

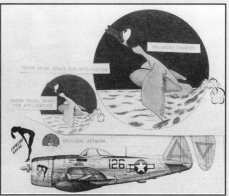

Here's another example of the artwork and the final decal before it was applied.

Top: the original artwork. Bottom: the color photocopy. Reduced to the proper scale size, the copy is very good quality.

• When you have your color copy in the correct size, cut it to shape and simply glue it to the airplane with a very thin coat of Pacer* Z-56 or aliphatic glue.

• After the glue has dried, spray on a coat of clear enamel. On a MonoKote* finish, you can seal the decal down with an overlay of clear MonoKote.

That's it! I used this technique to make the Red Baron Pizza decal for the tail of my ¼-scale Super Stearman and the nose art on my latest P-47 Thunderbolt. Give it a try; you'll like the results.

*Addresses are listed alphabetically in the Index of Manufacturers on page 146.

Paint checkerboards

by Curtis Mattikow

Nothing is more distinctive or visible than checkerboards. In addition to giving your aircraft that glamorous, aerobatic, barnstorming look, painting just the bottom or top really helps you orient the plane.

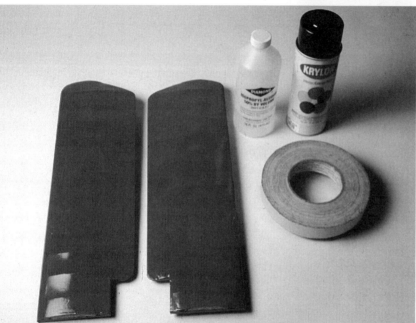

1 Cover or paint your surface with the lightest of your two (or three) colors. If you use paint as your base coat, be sure to give it at least a week to dry. Wipe the surface clean with alcohol. Choose tape whose width matches the size of your checkerboard squares. Tape in various widths is available at your local art-supply store; paper tape, electrical tape, or masking tape will do. Rubbing the sticky side of the tape against your jeans will reduce the tack somewhat and prevent you from removing previous paint coats when you pull off the tape.

2 Starting with the trailing edge, lay down spanwise strips of tape and use small, two-inch pieces of the same tape as spacers. Remove the spacers and save them for the next step.

3 Starting at the wing root, add a set of chordwise strips using the same system. Generally, wings look better with any odd-size squares at the leading edges and wingtips.

4 Remove the chordwise spacers, mask the outlying areas and spray on a few light coats. If you try to do this with one heavy coat, no matter what paint system you use, you're guaranteed to make a mess.

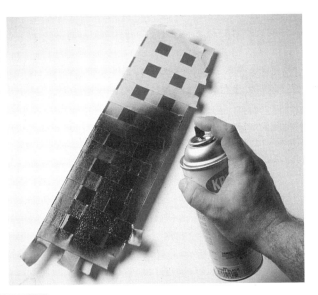

5 Remove the masking as soon as the last coat has set. At this point, you will have half the number of checkerboards. Wait at least one week for the paint to thoroughly harden, then apply tape directly over this fresh paint. Wipe clean with alcohol again to remove tape residue and fingerprints.

7 Spray again with a third color if desired. Carefully remove your masking and admire the results.

6 Apply masking again, but this time, apply it directly over the squares you have already painted, using them as your spacing guide.

8 For a matching touchup, spray some paint into a paper cup, let it thicken for a few minutes, and apply it with a small brush.

Prepping, priming, painting and detailing the aircraft
by David Sanders

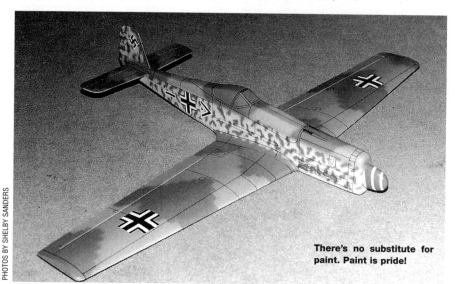

There's no substitute for paint. Paint is pride!

PHOTOS BY SHELBY SANDERS

Sometimes, film covering just won't do for a color scheme you really want. Or in the case of scale planes, you just can't explain away how the builders of the full-scale prototype were able to get 8x30-foot pieces of MonoKote*! That means it's gotta be paint. There's no substitute for paint. Paint is pride! When the boys at the field see a painted airplane roll up, they pay attention, don't they? Man, it sure would be cool to be able to do that intricate, mottled camo on your warbird or the fade-out edge stripes on a sport model, eh? Well, if

Materials required to build a good fiberglass base for a paint finish. I prefer Pacer* Z-poxy finishing resin.

you break the process down into simple steps, you can easily create fantastic paint work on your planes with minimum fuss, and I'm going to show you how.

THE MODEL
The model I'll be finishing in this article is of fully sheeted construction, although fabric-covered aircraft with open-bay framing are also easily completed with these methods. One major difference is that you must be certain to prep the fabric covering to accept paint per the fabric manufacturer's recommendations before proceeding. Also, you'll have to cut your masks before they're placed on the plane. This is a little more difficult, but not a huge inconvenience.

On wood-sheeted models, I always fiberglass the entire aircraft with at least ¾-ounce cloth and epoxy or polyester resin. For a super-light finish, I cover with silkspan and dope. Either way, you'll want to have the wood completely covered with one of these materials to provide a smooth, stable surface for painting. In the case of fiberglass, I cut the glass to cover the part, lightly spray it with 3M Super 77, lay it over the part, smooth it out and then apply the resin. I squeegee out excess resin with cardstock and get consistently lightweight glass jobs. In the June '96 *Model Airplane News*, Bob Fiorenze wrote an excellent article on glassing that provides detailed descriptions of every step necessary to get a good glass job.

This article will assume you're starting with a plane that is built and covered by one of these methods and is constructed up through final assembly.

BONDO FILLETS
On this small Dave's Aircraft Works* Focke-Wulf Ta152 slope glider, I wanted to have fillets at all the corners for a better scale look and in-flight perfor-

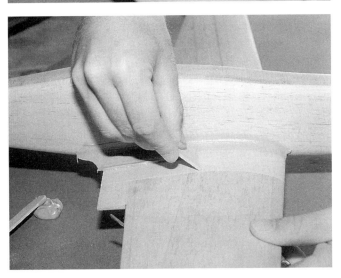

Top: cover the wing with masking tape so the fillet doesn't stick to the wing. Make trailing-edge fillet bases, being careful to get a good fit. Center: after applying the filler material, use a circular-tipped tool to form the fillet. Bottom: scrape excess filler off the wing and fuselage sides outside the fillet line.

mance. Good fillets can do a lot for your airplane's looks and performance, and since paint will easily follow any contour, I consider it a waste not to do the fillets on a plane I'm painting. On larger scale models, the wing fillets are usually part of the fuselage construction, but the Bondo method is still excellent for doing the tail surfaces, where applicable. Don't use spackle or model fillers, as they're way too soft and crumbly for this application. There are many automotive spot fillers available, so experiment a little. You're looking for stuff that is firm when cured and easy to sand.

Wrap the wing roots with masking tape to make sure the filler won't stick to them, then mount the wing on the plane.

Next, you'll want to make fillet bases to fit the trailing edge/fuselage area). I use 1/32- or 1/64-inch ply for these. You want these pieces to have a *very* good fit against the fuselage and wing. Don't worry about getting the corner radius perfect yet; cut it oversize. You'll bring the trailing edges of the fillets down to the correct radius at the end of the process. Glue these pieces to the fuselage with thick CA or epoxy, and leave a 1/64- to 1/32-inch gap at the wing trailing edge. You can support the fillet bases with a piece of masking tape on the bottom of the wing, too.

You'll need some sort of circular-tipped tool to form the fillets. A tongue depressor works great, as do Popsicle sticks for tighter radii. If you need an exact size, a piece of scrap balsa sheet can be quickly crafted into a suitable tool.

Mix up a generous batch of filler, then pack it into the corner so there are no bubbles or voids. Take particular care to get the filler into the tight corners at the fillet base, too. Only do one side of the wing at a time, and work quickly! The filler sets quickly, and it's a bear to form once it gets rubbery. Scrape out quite a bit of filler on the first batch, and don't worry about leaving too little behind. Scrape excess filler off the wing and fuselage sides outside the fillet line. You can also control the fillet width by rotating the tool as you pull it. Start at the front with the tool obliquely angled to the fuse side panel, then end with it perpendicular at the rear. This will yield a nice flared fillet. After the first pass sets up, mix another and repeat over the first layer. This time, pay attention to getting a smooth and true-to-form surface. I often use my fingers for this. At the wing leading edges, curl the fillet under to follow the wing. Sometimes, a third layer is appropriate, so use your judgment.

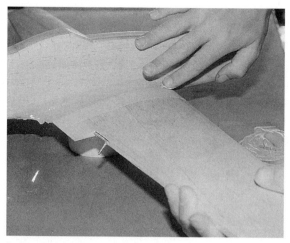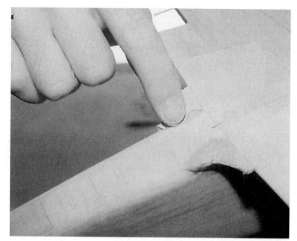

Left: after applying a second layer, use your finger to produce a smooth, true-to-form surface. Right: apply filler where the fillet bases meet the fuselage.

With both sides done on top of the plane, turn it over, and remove the tape that held the fillet bases in place during the previous steps. Apply filler where the fillet bases meet the fuselage. If your model has a belly scoop (as on a P-51), form the bottom fillets, too. These usually have a smaller

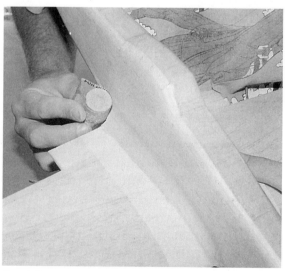

Use a suitable-size dowel; wrap a piece of sandpaper around it and sand your fillets smooth.

radius and are easier than the top fillets. Before the filler completely sets up, use your knife to cut through the fillet at the wing/fuse parting line.

You're almost to Nirvana … but you must sand! Sanding is Zen and must never be taken lightly! That said, use a suitable-size dowel or piece of tubing, wrap the sandpaper around it, and sand your fillets smooth. The Bondo sands well and is stiff enough to allow continued fine-tuning at this point. Now carefully sand the correct radius into the trailing edge of the fillets, and smooth the transition to the top of the wing. As the shape gets close to being finished, start using fine-grit paper

wrapped around your finger to really buff the Bondo smooth. Use more Bondo to fill any voids or pits at this stage, too. Carefully sand where the fillets meet the fuselage, and also try to get a consistent thickness over the wing panels where the fillet edges will be sanded to their final width.

Now the work pays off! Unbolt the wing, and carefully lift the trailing edge out of the fuselage. The Bondo might stick to the tape, but have faith; it will pop loose. The edges of the fillets will look raggedy, but resist the temptation to pick at 'em! Lay the fuselage on the bench, or place it in a stand, bottom up. With scrap glass cloth (1-ounce weight or less), cut some strips to lay over the wing-mating surface of the fillets. Spray these on one side with Super 77, then place them on the fillets, letting the edges run out past the outboard edge and into the fuselage cavity. Squirt the cloth with thin CA, and let it cure thoroughly. This makes the fillets very strong. Trim the cloth flush to the fuselage cavity

Carefully sand the correct radius into the trailing edge of the fillets.

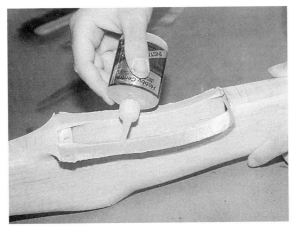

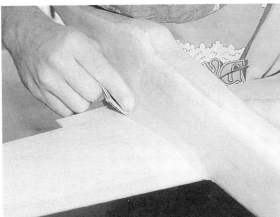

Top: with scrap glass cloth (1-ounce weight or less), cut some strips to lay over the wing-mating surface of the fillets, gluing them in place with thin CA. Center: once the edges have been cleaned up, bolt the wing back onto the fuselage and fine-sand the fillets one last time. Bottom: use the same techniques on the tail surfaces.

opening, and rough-cut the fillets' outboard edges with your knife or razor saw. Turn the fuselage back over, and mark the finish width on the fillets. Carefully sand the edges of the fillets to the lines with a *hard* sanding block. A piece of ¾-inch parti-

cle-board sanding block works great. Once the edges have been cleaned up, bolt the wing back onto the fuse, and fine-sand the fillets one last time.

Now you have great-looking fillets on the wings. I use similar techniques at the tail, and it's actually much easier since these surfaces are usually permanently attached to the plane. Soon, you'll find you can make your all-wood aircraft have the shapely lines of much more expensive molded glass jobs.

PRIMING

I get great satisfaction from seeing my model's shape in an all-white color with only its smooth surface contours evident. One of the reasons is that I get a chance to see any and all defects and correct them prior to shooting color.

Plasti-Kote sandable primer is an absolute must-have in my shop. This stuff is amazing and has saved my life as a model airplane painter after my previous favorite was reformulated and ruined! Don't substitute unless you're certain your primer sands well, as it can make or break your paint job.

Spray a generous coat of primer on your bird. Now sand it almost completely off with 220-grit, aluminum-oxide, open-coat paper. This fills the tiny imperfections in your glass job and ensures that you haven't left any standing weave or seams. You'll immediately notice how smooth the surface feels after this step.

Spray a second coat, but not as heavy as the first. Sand with 220-grit until it gets "hazy" or semi-transparent.

Spray a light third coat that gives good coverage. Sand it lightly with 320- to 400-grit paper. This is the final primer coat and your last defense against the error-magnifying color coats to come, so inspect it carefully and prime again if necessary.

The completion of priming is a milestone in your model's life. Enjoy it, because its shape will never be this perfect again!

The completion of priming is a milestone in your model's life. Enjoy it, because its shape will never be this perfect again!

PRELIMINARY PANEL LINING

Now that you have a primed, ready-to-paint aircraft, it's time to get some war paint on that beauty.

Full-scale aircraft painters often use panel lines for alignment of markings, and the fuselage will usually have at least one panel line that runs nearly from nose to tail. Use a sharp pencil and straightedge to lightly mark one on the model. Carefully establish the exact height of its endpoints so it can act as a datum for the others. It's just dark enough to faintly see it through the paint when applied. Wings and tail surfaces are done similarly. Only do enough lines to properly align insignias, stripes, or camouflage boundaries. As you proceed with painting, go over them with the pencil as required to ensure visibility through the entire process.

AIRBRUSHES AND PAINT RAP

My techniques work with nearly any paint, but I prefer flat enamels, like Testor's* Model Master enamels. What you're looking for is fast

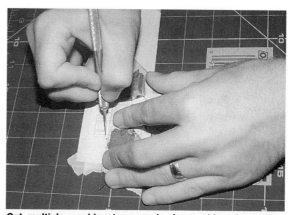

Draw a data line that runs from nose to tail to orient markings.

drying, resistance to peeling with masking tape and easy clean-up. Also, be sure the paint is compatible with your clear coat, which determines the final finish gloss and protects against fuel, handling, etc.

I've used several airbrushes and, for large models, automotive "touch-up" guns. Touch-up guns can cost a lot, but airbrushes are fairly reasonably priced. I've recently acquired a Badger* 200 that's excellent for camouflaging, and it's used for this project. All my airbrushes are "single-action"; the

trigger button controls the air only. A "double-action" gun's staged trigger button shoots air independently, then with further movement, paint. Single-action guns are easier to use and clean, so I recommend them. I use an air compressor with a pressure valve and water trap. You can buy compressed air in cans for small models, but if you're painting gigantic beasts, you'll want a compressor.

Always have a supply of compatible thinner on hand! I have three airbrush bottles available during a painting project; one of them contains thinner. I use this bottle to "quick-clean" the gun when taking breaks or switching colors. You'll need to thin the paint for the gun; generally, gloss requires more thinning. Most glosses need a 1:1 mix, but flats usually use a 2:1 paint-to-thinner ratio. Test the gun on white card stock to find the best ratio. You want the paint to cover well but not look "cakey" (too thick). Nor should it be thin and runny. In addition to the instructions for your gun, there are many books available to help you get the best performance from your gun/paint combination.

Cut multiple masking tape masks for markings by cutting through several layers of tape.

Here, the marking masks are in place, waiting for paint.

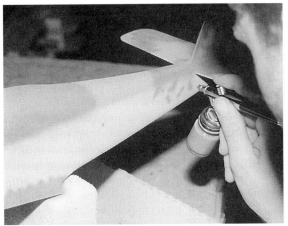

Mottled camouflage is easy to do with an airbrush, but practice on card stock to establish proper mottle density and size.

When painting different camouflage colors, shoot the boundaries between the two colors first, then fill in the rest.

couple of coats, and paint well outside where the white will show.

Now mask anywhere there's white on the finished model. When cutting Maltese crosses and such insignia from a stack of masking tape on a vinyl cutting mat, a printout of the insignia can be laid over the tape to guide cutting. Though the cross will have only thin, white lines inside a black field, mask the entire cross; the same goes for the rank chevrons, gruppe bars and swastikas. Notice careful alignment with the penciled panel lines.

Never use the factory edge of the tape. Even if you're masking straight lines, cut the tape lengthwise with a straightedge so the edge is clean. This will leave crisp color separations.

Like most military aircraft, this scheme uses very light gray that covers the bottom surfaces of the airframe, the fin and about ⅔ up the fuselage sides. Get coverage a little beyond where the darker colors overlap. Shoot the next darker color, the lightest of the camouflage colors on the upper surfaces. I freehand the color separation on the side of the fuselage, but you can

Finally, there's clear coat. I like Varathane Polyurethane, which comes in gloss or satin and is packaged in aerosol cans or brush cans. If using the brush type, be sure to get some compatible thinner so you can shoot it through the gun. On military models, I use the satin type in an aerosol can. For a gloss finish, it's best to clear coat with the gun, which gives a more uniform film. For power planes, good ol' K&B*, which imparts a thick, chip- and fuel-resistant coating, is still my favorite.

MASKING AND PAINTING
The secret to vibrant color on your models is to shoot light colors first, then progressively darker colors after that, with only few exceptions. This seems obvious but can mean challenges when masking. Planning ahead is crucial to success! On this model, I shot a patch of white anywhere that white occurred in the final scheme. Use at least a

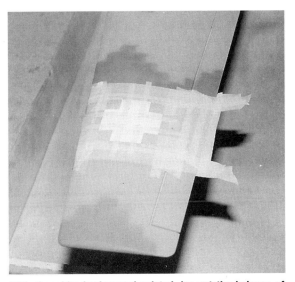

With the white background painted, lay out the balance of the Maltese crosses so you can spray the black part of the markings.

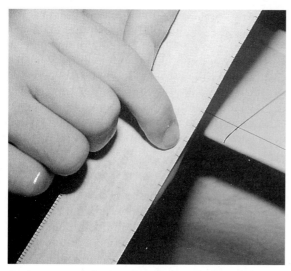

An important tool when doing panel lines is a flexible, plastic straightedge. Apply a layer of masking tape to the back of the straightedge so that it's raised off the surface while drawing a line.

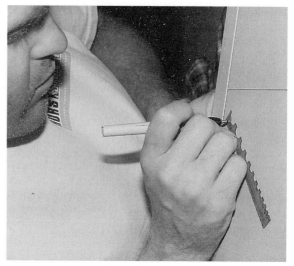

Cutting up drafting templates to use as pen guides produces some very useful tools for panel creation.

use a piece of card stock held ½ inch or so away from the plane and shoot across it, too. This will still yield a nice fade-out edge. The wavy line at the fillet is also freehanded. Practice fade-out edges on white card stock to get a feel for it, and adjust the gun for best results. After you're in the groove, do the plane.

Next, shoot the dark camouflage and the mottling. On camouflage, carefully shoot the boundaries between lighter and darker colors, then fill in the rest. If the camouflage creeps from wing to fuselage, shoot it with the wings and fuselage joined to ensure a good match.

Mottles are something you definitely want to "warm up to" on a piece of white card stock. Experiment with different motions to get the effect you want. After you're "grooved in," shoot the plane immediately, while you've got the rhythm. Don't stop until the first coat of mottling is complete. It will look different every time depending on your beer or coffee level that day.

I shoot each color in two coats. It's pretty easy to maintain control and not overshoot the first coat by using low paint volume. If you're lucky and get good coverage with the first coat, you won't need a second, but usually it takes two.

With the basic colors complete, let's turn our attention to the insignias. For Maltese crosses, use square tape pieces to mask the inside corners, then mask the ends of the bars, and finally, use thin strips to mask the white lines. The previously masked-out white area defines the dimensions of the cross and serves as a masking guide. The strips are laid in a tic-tac-toe grid, then the middle square is carefully cut out, leaving four L-shaped

legs. Use butcher paper to mask the rest of the plane so that no overspray gets on the camouflage, then shoot the black. On the fuselage, mask the white edges of the rank and *gruppe* markings, too. I don't attempt to paint the black in the swastika on small models; I do that with ink while panel lining.

The spinner was completely masked during camouflaging, then a tape strip was spiral-wrapped around it prior to shooting the light blue. The white field of the *Udet Gruppe* badge was done the same and a carefully cut mask laid over it to shoot the red.

Now, there are exceptions to the "dark over light" rule. Canopy glazing is one. It's easier to mask the glazing boundaries than the glazed area itself. This necessitates shooting a light color over dark camouflage. For this, mask the glazing boundaries, then apply a coat of white prior to the final color, allowing it to dry thoroughly. Then

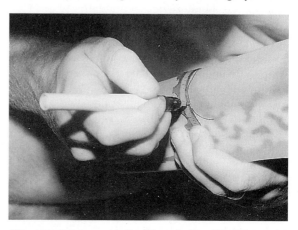

These templates are very flexible and will pull tight to curved surfaces.

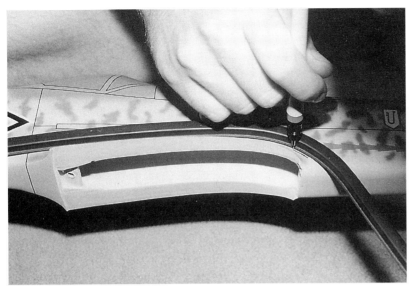

Here, a flexible curve tool is used to draw the fillet panel edge.

you'll get good coverage with as few as two coats of the glazing color. The rust-colored exhaust stacks were done the same way. U.S. insignias are another place where this technique is useful. Mask out the white star and bars, then shoot a patch of insignia blue over that. Next, apply a mask shaped like the blue outer boundary of the insignia, which stays in place until the plane has been completely painted.

After the model has dried thoroughly, wipe it down with a soft cotton cloth to

◼ The Badger Model 200 Airbrush

Over the course of the project depicted here, I had the pleasure of laying down paint with the Badger Model 200 Airbrush. For you total tool nuts, it's a bottom-feed, single-action, internal-mix gun.

This gun is well-suited to the aeromodeler's needs. First, it's bottom-fed, which allows you to use as large or as small a paint canister as you'd like. I typically will use a 6-ounce canister when shooting primer but can still switch to a 1-ounce canister for shooting small details. In addition to this, it gives the gun a low center of gravity so that it rests easily in your hand, allowing you to relax. It's impossible to get a good finish if you're tensed up, worrying about spills, as you would be with a top-fed gun.

Second, it's single-action. This means the trigger button controls air only, and paint siphon-feeds from the canister. Double-action guns are far more difficult to get a "feel" for and are a lot of trouble to clean. The single-action gun can usually give a neophyte airbrusher good results since its operation closely resembles the spray cans he or she is graduating up from. The trigger-button spring tension is light but not sloppy, and I can paint for hours without getting a cranky trigger finger.

The gun comes stock with a large-gauge spray regulator tip, although Badger offers medium and fine regulator tips for very detailed work. So far, I've been able to get as fine a spray pattern as I've ever needed with the large-gauge tip while still being able to "open

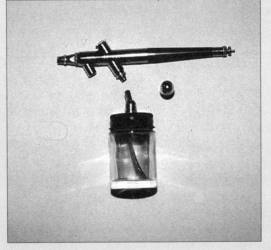

up" the gun and cover large areas if necessary.

Paint volume is controlled by a knob at the butt of the handle; this keeps your adjustment hand well away from the tip while you're adjusting the spray. This may seem trivial, but it only takes one episode of not noticing the errant paint on your finger from fooling with a tip-adjusted gun, then laying a big, fat fingerprint on your project to help you appreciate this feature! Adjustment is very silky and positive and stays correct with no tendency to "stray."

Fit and finish of all the components are absolutely outstanding, and the gun feels very nice in your hand. The chrome-plated head discourages paint adhesion, making it easy to clean.

Included with the gun is an excellent owner's manual that can get you off on the right foot, discussing adjustment, cleaning and maintenance, as well as techniques to achieve the best finish and effects. Also included are tips for thinning to allow the best results with a variety of media, as well as a troubleshooting section to help you target and correct common gun setup problems.

I found this gun a pleasure to use, and it has given me many hours of trouble-free use with virtually no maintenance other than regular cleaning. If you want a serious gun that will allow you to achieve professional-quality finishes, I'd highly recommend the Badger Model 200.

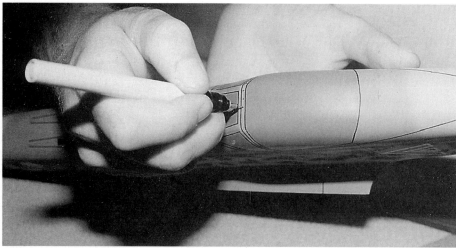

Rivets are easily simulated by stippling.

knock down standing paint at masked edges and tiny flecks of dust. This is analogous to "sanding" but doesn't really cut the paint. It will buff to a very slight gloss during this procedure. After that, shoot one clear coat. With a couple more clear coats, you could be done. If you want to follow along for the panel lines, though, shoot one coat of satin, and let it dry overnight.

PANEL LINING WITH PENS

For the very best results, Rapidographs, or "technical" pens, can't be beat. These are fine instruments and come in a wide range of qualities and sizes. I use standard tungsten nibs on my pens, which work fine; you don't need the expensive jewel tips for this. My favorite ink is Higgins Black Magic, which really lives up to its name! It sticks well, is very opaque and dries quickly. It goes flat when dry, so it's easy to tell whether it's wet so you don't smudge it. The best part is water cleanup. And you can leave it in your pens for weeks without clogging.

Another important tool is a flexible, plastic straightedge. It will follow curved surfaces easily, and it won't mar your finish.

Also used are plastic drafting templates. I'll often cut up templates to make special shapes, such as a clipped circle template for the radiused corners of an access panel. These templates are very flexible and will pull tight curves.

Hold the Rapidograph perpendicular to the work surface. The ink will not flow unless the pen's valve is opened by a fine wire at the center of the nib. This requires that the pen be kept perpendicular to the surface.

A flexible curve tool can be used to draw the fillet panel edge. This drafting tool is very handy and can be bent into any curve. Also visible are the painted exhaust stacks. After pen outlining, they will have a striking scale appearance, even though they're flat.

Rivets are simulated by stippling. I just eyeball the spacings by doing "landmark" rivets first, like the ends and center points of panel lines, then filling in with progressively tighter spacings. Don't go crazy, as overdoing rivets can spoil the scale illusion. Use them sparingly as a highlighting effect. Also, you can see that the canopy glazing is outlined, which really makes it "pop."

For radiused corners, the circle templates work well. Always do the corners first, then fill in the straight lines. This ensures the best straight-to-curve transitions.

During panel lining, keep a damp (not wet) cloth handy for wiping off the pen nib, tools ... and mistakes! If you catch errors quickly, you can "erase" with the damp cloth.

As a last step, carefully draw in the black part of the swastikas, leaving a thin band of white paint showing to create the outline.

FINAL TOUCHES

Dust the model off, then shoot another clear coat. After curing, do the cotton cloth wipe-down, then shoot another coat or two. With a satin finish model, you're done! In the case of a gloss finish, buff it again with car wax after the clear coat has cured for a few days.

The more you paint, the better and quicker you'll get. Pretty soon, you'll be able to reproduce any scale color scheme you desire and replicate unusual markings you could never get on a decal sheet; plus you'll have the pride of saying, "It's paint! Every bit of it!"

Addresses are listed alphabetically in the Index of Manufacturers on page 146.

Using Liquid Masking Film

by Jim Sandquist

After a decade of modeling, I thought I knew nearly all the best products on the market. But recently, I used Bob Dively's* Liquid Masking Film for the first time. This product has been around for years, but I never had the need to try it until I modeled the P-51, "Big Beautiful Doll." The problem was how to apply a checkerboard nose and get straight lines over my panel lines and Duz fasteners. This product really did the job! Give it a try the next time you have a tough masking job. Liquid Masking Film can be used over any non-porous surface and will leave razor-sharp edges over compound curves, panel lines, etc. It's available in 4-, 16- and 32-ounce bottles.

1 Brush or spray the Liquid Mask onto the surface to be painted. There is no problem with applying the mask over your base color; the Mask has no adhesive and cannot lift the base-color paint. For best results, let it dry overnight.

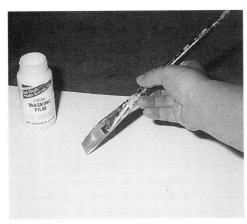

2 Draw your pattern right on top of the film! If you can draw it, you can mask it!

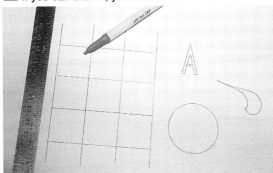

3 Use a hobby knife to carefully cut out the area you want to be a different color than your base. Very little pressure is required to cut the film. Now lift away the film from the areas to be painted.

4 Use an airbrush or spray paint. The areas you don't want painted will be protected by the film.

5 The images are crisp and clean with no flashing. The excess Liquid Masking Film lifts right off! I didn't have any paint compatibility problems, but always test with your paint first.

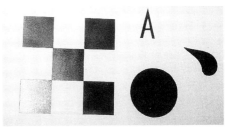

*Addresses are listed alphabetically in the Index of Manufacturers on page 146. ✦

U.S. Army Air Corps colors and markings

Text and illustrations by Jim Newman

■ U.S. ARMY PAINT SCHEMES

Paint schemes and markings on military aircraft varied considerably as the years passed, often seemingly without any real logic behind the changes. This leads me to wonder if markings and camouflage are similar to fashion: subject to the whims of those in power at the time. It is known, however, that on both sides of the Atlantic, departments exist wherein a team of color specialists concocts mixes of paint that

supposedly render aircraft difficult to see or, when applied in carefully "designed" patterns and combinations, distort the outline sufficiently to make the observer wonder if he really saw what he thought he saw! Yes, camouflage does work, as long as the aircraft to which it is applied remains over the background for which the scheme was designed, and this hardly ever happens.

The following notes offer some guidance as to the changes in colors and markings as the years progressed. Be advised that when building a scale model, one should work according to some kind of specific documentation, i.e., photographs, drawings and descriptions of the type of aircraft being modeled, because there were always some deviations or exceptions to the schemes mentioned.

• **Pre-1918.** Aircraft supplied to the U.S. Army Air Corps by U.S. manufacturers prior to WW I were generally devoid of any paint scheme. They generally had just a clear-doped-linen finish. Because the raw, undoped fabric was a very pale oatmeal color, the clear-doped fabric took on a translucent, grayish-cream look and, in model fabrics, the Antique Super Coverite very closely approximates this.

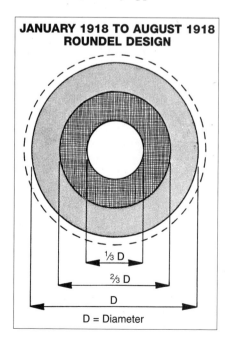

JANUARY 1918 TO AUGUST 1918 ROUNDEL DESIGN

⅓ D

⅔ D

D

D = Diameter

Under-wing lettering for most trainers was 24 inches tall. Though the above photo clearly shows the angled corners of the letters, there were times when the lettering was rounded by manufacturers.

Exceptions: aircraft supplied by foreign sources retained the factory paint scheme applied. The British de Havilland 4 retained its dark green top, sides and fin (including the fuselage underside). Wings and stabilizer had clear-doped undersides. The French Nieuport was all silver. SPAD fighters had tan and dark green camouflage sides and upper surfaces with clear-doped undersides.

• **1918.** The Army Air Corps standardized the color scheme. Until 1927, the order was olive drab upper surfaces. The vertical surfaces and fuselage undersides had clear-doped finishes, although sometimes, the fuselage sides were given a protective coat of pale cream. The bottoms of wings and horizontal stabilizers were clear-doped.

The olive drab, or "OD," as it became commonly known, of that era was vastly different from the OD of today and of that offered by current model-covering materials that are more of a brown shade. The early OD had a definite greenish look to it and closely matched the Olive Drab FS 34087 published in the Federal Standard (FS) 595 dated March 1, 1956; if you have a copy with that date on it, you had better keep it under lock and key, because it's priceless. Examination of good photos of that time produced from glass-plate negatives show the paints to be anything from matte to semi-matte.

• **1927.** The military developed concerns over air-to-air collisions. The army specified that wings, horizontal tails, fins and rudders must be finished in Chrome Yellow FS 3358—a semi-matte color close to Cub Yellow or FS 33538. Struts and landing gear were also finished in OD.

• **1928.** The Army took delivery of its first all-metal aircraft—the Ford Trimotor—and specified that all transport aircraft were to be delivered in natural metal. But in 1935, the Northrop Co. delivered a painted A-17 aircraft, and they remained painted until 1936.

• **1936.** The Army specified a gloss Light Blue FS 15102 (ANA 501) for all fuselages except the metal-skinned machines, which were to be supplied in natural metal. The new metal-skinned Northrop A-17A was an exception and was painted gloss Light Blue. The natural-metal finish on other metal-skinned machines was retained until 1941. Other exceptions were: Ryan PT-16, -20, -21, -22

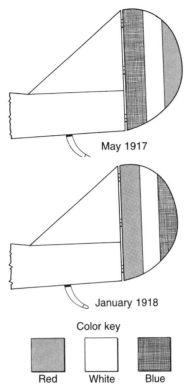

EARLY RUDDER DETAIL

May 1917

January 1918

Color key

Red   White   Blue

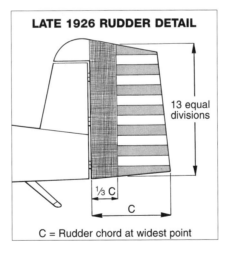

LATE 1926 RUDDER DETAIL

13 equal divisions

⅓ C

C

C = Rudder chord at widest point

with natural-metal fuselage, chrome yellow wing, stabilizer and fin.

• **1940.** Many obsolescent combat aircraft were relegated to training duties and were required to be painted silver overall or to remain in natural metal with silver-painted fabric surfaces. New aircraft were to be delivered in OD with the undersides in Neutral Gray FS 36173. (The Twin Beech C-45 was the only transport aircraft remaining in blue and yellow, but it eventually changed schemes, with many special-purpose schemes as WW II escalated.)

• **1941.** The night-fighter scheme was adopted for the converted Douglas A-20. It was matte black overall. Later, the P-61 and the F-82 were painted gloss black overall. The B-29 remained in natural metal and was used at night; its underside was painted gloss black with a wavy demarcation line along the fuselage side.

• **Early 1942.** The blue-and-yellow scheme was deleted from all training aircraft, and silver overall was made standard for these types, although many did survive the War still in their blue and yellow.

• **May 1942.** For air operations in North Africa, OD was replaced by Desert Sand FS 30279, which is seen on P-40s and some B-24s. The neutral gray undersides were replaced by Azure Blue FS 35231.

Planes delivered from Britain did not follow these color schemes. They were operated in their original Dark Earth FS 30118 and Dark Green FS 34079 RAF camouflage; British markings were painted over with a circle and star. RAF code letters and serial numbers were often retained. Some British aircraft, e.g., the Hurricane and the Spitfire, were delivered in RAF desert camouflage of Dark Earth FS 30118 and Middle Stone FS 30266 with the Azure Blue undersides.

• **1944.** Camouflage was deleted, except on liaison types (L-4, L-5, etc.), helicopters and night fighters.

THE MARKINGS PROGRESSION

• **May 19, 1917.** U.S. Army Air Corps adopted the star in a blue circle with a red dot in the center. This was applied inboard of the ailerons and ran the full chord of the upper surface of the top wing and the lower surface of the bottom wing. Three stripes of equal width were on the rudder—blue at the leading edge, white in the center and red at the trailing edge. Note: the blue was considerably lighter than the Insignia Blue of 1941 and varied considerably in shade owing to non-standardization.

• **January 1918 to August 1919.** USAAC adopted the red, white and blue roundels, especially on the war front in Europe. Within the U.S., many aircraft retained the star, but some carried a mixture of the two markings well into 1919. This was primarily caused by repairs and the swapping of components between aircraft. It was not unusual to see one aircraft carrying roundels and stars— even on opposite wings! The order of the vertical rudder

STAR IN CIRCLE DETAIL

Yellow May 1942 to April 1943

1/8 R

May 19, 1917   Late May 1942

Top: star in circle detail. Center: the Northrop A-17 carries the Army-specified gloss blue fuselage that was retained until 1941. Note the early white-star-in-blue-circle insignia with red center markings. Bottom: at the Ryan Aeronautical Co. plant in San Diego, CA, a huge number of Ryan PT-21 army trainers and NR-1 Navy trainers await shipment to training units throughout the country. Circa 1936, natural-metal fuselage, chrome yellow wings, stab and fin. Rudder has blue leading edge with 13 red and white horizontal stripes.

STAR-AND-BAR DETAIL

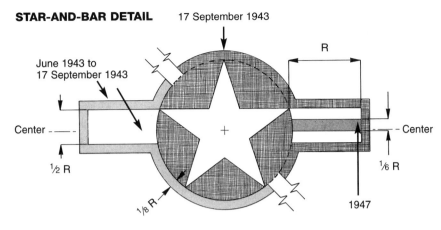

Note: white bar is not centered on center of circle

Here, an all-olive-drab P-40 wears the star-and-blue-circle insignia with red center painted over. The nose and tail numbers were probably yellow. In May 1942, for air operations in North Africa, olive drab finishes were replaced with Desert Sand FS 30279. The neutral gray underside was also replaced with Azure Blue FS 35231.

stripes reversed, with red now at the leading edge and blue at the trailing edge.

• **After 1919.** Aircraft returned to the star in a circle.

• **Late 1926.** A pattern of 13 alternating red and white rudder stripes was adopted, along with a single blue vertical rudder stripe.

• **End of February 1941.** There was a major change to the national insignia. The red-and-white tail stripes were deleted from the rudder of combat aircraft. A white star on an Insignia Blue FS 35044 disk was applied to each side of the fuselage—top of left wing and underside of right wing. Uncamouflaged aircraft retained stars on the top and bottom of both wings.

A curious reason was given for the asymmetric application of the wing stars. It was feared that

CONSTRUCTING THE STAR

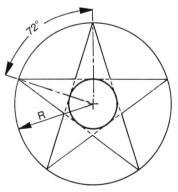

R = Radius

enemy pilots would use them as ranging marks based on the distance between the stars. Having been involved with gun-sight trials, the idea of using national insignia for ranging caused me no end of mirth, because most gun sights were calibrated in terms of the target aircraft wingspans, not the distance between crosses or "meatballs," which could vary! It was obviously some high-ranking officer's muddled thinking that was caused by combat fatigue and aggravated by too many hours flying a heavily armed desk.

• **Early 1942.** Red-and-white tail stripes were deleted from all aircraft.

• **End of May 1942.** Red dot deleted from the center of the star.

• **Until June 1942.** Aircraft that were not camouflaged continued to carry stars on both wings.

• **May 1942 to April 1943.** Some aircraft operating out of England and in North Africa carried a 2-inch-wide circle of Yellow FS 3358 surrounding the dark blue background of the star.

• **Early 1943.** Asymmetric application of wing stars was adopted for all types of aircraft.

• **June 1943 to 17 September 1943.** A white bar was added to each side of the dark blue disk, and the whole insignia was outlined in Insignia Red FS 30109 (the same dull red that had been adopted for the center of the RAF insignia).

The white bar was not centered in the circle but was aligned with the upper edge of the horizontal points of the star.

• **17 September 1943.** The red outline was painted over with the Insignia Blue FS 35044.

• **1947.** A Red FS 31136 bar was added to each white bar.

LETTERING

• **1927 to end of May 1942.** "U.S. ARMY" was written in large letters across the underside of the bottom wings on biplanes and across the underside of monoplane wings (see illustration for proportions). On most trainers, letters were 24 inches tall; black letters on gray, silver or yellow. Many aircraft still carried this lettering until well after 1942. Although the illustration shows letters with angled corners, some manufacturers applied letters with rounded corners, so check your reference photos!

Technical data was carried on a panel that was low on the fuselage's left side; depending on the type of aircraft, it was below or forward of the cockpit. Lettering described aircraft type, serial number, fuel and oil requirements, etc., and was, at most, 1 inch tall. Letters were black, white, or yellow on blue, or they were black, white, or yellow on OD.

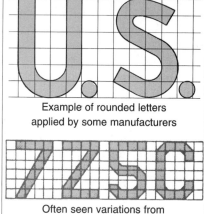

A rare Republic TP-47G Thunderbolt (two-place trainer version) is dressed with the blue-and-white star-and-bars insignia. The overall finish is olive drab with a neutral gray underside.

BLOCK LETTER STYLE

Layout of standard block letters 3:2 height/width ratio 45° corners

Example of rounded letters applied by some manufacturers

Often seen variations from the official specifications

In these variations, the letter C with the extended ends, the 7 and Z, without the 45° corners, are more pleasant to view than the official style! Check your documentation.

OFFICIAL LETTERING STYLES

ABCDEFGHIJ
KLMNOPQRS
TUVWXYZ
1234567890

(From USAF Manual T.O. 1-1-4 Exterior Finished Insignia & Markings Applicable to USAF Aircraft)

Width of letters = 2/3 height
M & W width = height
Stroke thickness = 1/6 height
Space between letters = 1/6 height
Space between words = 2/3 height

Here, a B-25 Mitchell bomber displays the typical star-and-bars U.S. insignia with red painted around the insignia.

An all-silver Aeronca L-16A with thin red stripes added to the white bars of the U.S. insignia—circa 1947.

The above material is from a variety of sources so, again, the author urges builders to check aircraft being modeled against reliable references such as photographs.

Apply painted markings

by Stephen Philbrick

R ecently, my brother Whit and I built a ⅕-scale IMP* FW 190D. Since we were interested in scale competition, we decided that a painted finish, including the various markings and insignia, was necessary to be competitive. Decals (if available for the subject aircraft) can speed the finishing process, but they leave a raised edge around the marking and limit the amount of weathering you can do to the model.

Painted markings, on the other hand, allowed us to weather the various markings and insignia along with the rest of the finish for a more realistic appearance. And, the markings are thinner (only as thick as the paint), are fuelproof and do not need a clear top coat.

To begin with, I'd suggest practicing the technique before you apply it to your finished model. Here's how we did our markings.

This FW 190 has a painted finish including all the scale markings. Decals might make the job easier, but painted markings and insignia allow the entire finish to be weathered for an authentic appearance.

1 Prepare for the task by studying scale documentation for your model. Here, we are using the Squadron/Signal Publications* book "Walk Around FW 190D" as a reference for color and markings. A proportional scale is useful in determining the proper scale factor to enlarge the various markings shown in the book to the size required for our model. Different scaling ratios may be required if markings are shown in the book at various scale sizes.

2 Using the proper scale ratio, enlarge the markings from the book to the size needed for your model. You can use a flatbed scanner to digitally enlarge the marking, or you can use a photocopier to enlarge it several times until you have the size required. Check the final enlargement against other "landmarks" on your model (hatches and panel lines) for proper size.

We used Frisk-It material, available at art supply stores, to make the painting template. We traced the markings from the enlargement using a dark colored pen. It may be necessary to correct for distortions to the marking caused by the enlargement process. Use a straightedge and make sure that the lines are straight or parallel where required.

3 Remove the masking material from its backing paper and carefully position it on the model. Make sure that the surface of the model is clean and dust-free. Smooth the masking material into place by gently rubbing it to remove any air bubbles trapped beneath it.

We cut the masking material using a sharp no. 11 hobby blade after the mask has been applied to the model. This way, you get a cleaner cut line and in general, it is easier to apply the material before openings are cut into it. Now carefully remove the unwanted portion of the mask. Cover the rest of the model with newspaper or wrapping paper and tape it into place around the masking material. Used masking tape is good for this, as it is less tacky than new tape and there is less chance of damaging the finish when it is removed.

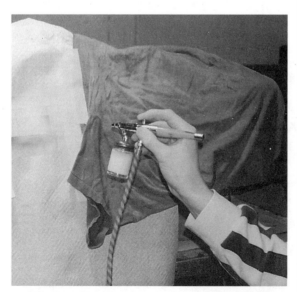

4 When spraying the markings, seal the edges of the mask with a light coat of paint. Allow a minute or two for the paint to settle, then follow this with broad, even strokes of paint to finish the marking. Wait until the paint has dried but not completely hardened before peeling off the mask. Remove the mask slowly and carefully, making sure not to touch the painted area.

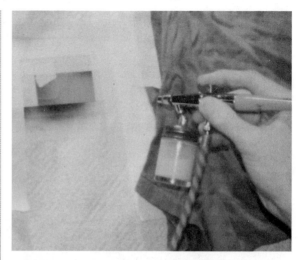

5 For multicolored markings, start with the lightest color paint then add the darker portions after the previous color has completely dried. Apply the mask for each color and repeat the process. When the last color has been applied, remove the mask and wait for it to completely harden, then do any touchup work or weathering. Before the paint completely hardens, you can remove any imperfections with a small amount of solvent applied with a paper towel or a cotton swab. You might also want to use this technique to blend or dull the edges of the markings, depending on the effect you are trying to create. Remember: not all markings on warbirds were picture perfect; some were hastily applied in the field by hand or with rough-cut templates.

6 Here, the completed triangle markings are finished. The number 1, as well as all the other markings on the FW 190, were applied in the same way. The finished model looks great and when weathered, the effect should be very pleasing and look quite authentic.

Addresses are listed alphabetically in the Index of Manufacturers on page 146.

Create razor-sharp graphics

by Ed Smetak

Many model-ers believe that letter-perfect custom graphics are beyond their budgets or capabilities. After countless hours of building, they settle for a few "off-the-shelf" decals or leave their aircraft plain and boring.

With the techniques presented here, you'll have everything you need to create strikingly sharp custom graphics that will certainly turn heads; the best part is that it's inexpensive and easy, too!

The first step is to create a full-size pattern on a piece of lightweight paper (paper lighter than the standard 20-pound is easier to cut through). You can create a pattern for your graphic however you want—even draw it by hand. I use a personal computer and Microsoft Windows' Paint (in the Accessories folder). You work with lines, shapes, text, styles and sizes, and you can experiment with different color schemes—even zoom in and edit the image pixel by pixel! When you've finished designing, print out your pattern on a piece of the lightweight paper. Printing the pattern in light gray rather than black makes it easier to see exactly where the point of the knife is during the cutting process.

Next attach the pattern directly to the fuel-resistant vinyl trim sheet material with masking tape. You don't want your design to shift around even the slightest bit while you're cutting it.

Working on a well-lit surface, cut through the pattern and the trim material using the X-Acto knife—but not all the way through the protective backing. You'll quickly learn how much pressure it requires to accomplish this. Consider picking up an X-Acto no. X3241. This knife's swivel blade rotates 360 degrees for cutting curves, circles and designs. You'll wonder how you ever worked without it. If you do cut all the way through the protective backing in some areas, don't worry, as long as the backing is still in one piece and holds the design together. It's imperative to use a sharp blade! If you notice even the slightest pulling as you cut, change the blade; this will keep the edges of your graphic sharp. Take your time cutting out your design. A little time and patience will go a long way. Cut a curve, then lay your straightedge against the blade to cut a straight section, then a curve, and so on. Discard the paper pattern and "weed" out the background trim material with your knife and tweezers as you go. If you must stop cutting, be careful to get the blade back exactly

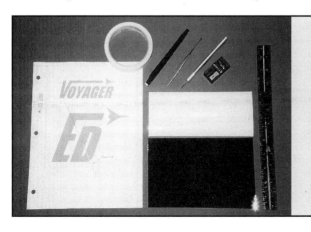

MATERIALS

- Full-size copy of graphic.
- Lightweight paper (less than 20 lb.).
- Self-adhesive trim sheet (fuel-resistant).
- X-Acto knife and no. 11 blades, and X-Acto no. 3241 craft swivel knife (optional).
- Fine-point felt-tip pen.
- Masking tape.
- Sharp tweezers.
- Straightedge.
- Clear or semitransparent application tape.
- Post-It note pad (for use on dark-colored models).
- Clear dope and brush.

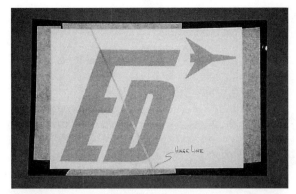

The printed graphic is taped into place over the trim sheet.

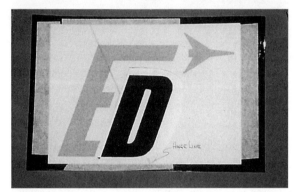

Carefully cut the pattern with an X-Acto knife. The material in and around the "D" has been "weeded out."

where you left off before you continue.

Mark guidelines on your model using a felt-tip pen where the graphic will be placed. For dark-colored models, mark temporary guidelines using those little yellow stick-on notes.

Transfer the graphic from its protective backing to your model using application tape (available in various sizes from any vinyl-sign-making shop or art-supply store). Stick the application tape over your graphic. Carefully peel the application tape from the trim sheet's protective backing; the graphic will now adhere to the application tape. Be particularly careful not to crease the graphic by bending it back too far or pulling it up too quickly. Creases won't smooth out after the graphic has been applied; you'll have to cut a new one.

Remove the graphic from its protective backing with application tape.

Take your time, use your guidelines (transparent application tape makes it easier to see your guidelines), and gently lay the graphic down on the surface with a continuous, smooth motion, being careful not to trap air bubbles underneath. If you do trap a bubble, carefully pierce the graphic with the tip of your knife and smooth it out.

After the graphic has been applied, burnish it with a soft cloth. Carefully pull off the application tape by bending it back on itself while pulling up slowly (you don't want to pull the covering off your plane!). Use a trim-sealing iron set on low to lay graphics over the edges of a hinge slot.

Now wipe off the guidelines with a damp cloth. To prevent fuel from seeping under the graphic, brush some clear dope around its edges or clearcoat it entirely. That's it; step back and admire your work!

I am always interested in exchanging ideas with other R/C modelers. I am a member of the Jetero R/C Club in Houston, TX; www.jetero.org. Feel free to drop me a note at ecsmetak@king-woodcable.com, or visit my website at www.smetak.com. ✦

Above: position the graphic and smooth it into place. Below: remove the application tape and seal the hinge line's edges.

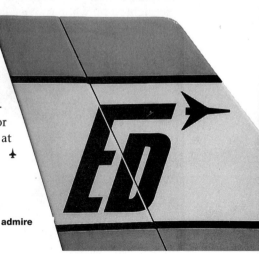

Step back and admire your work!

Apply polished-aluminum panels by Terry Nitsch

Simulating aluminum skin on scale-model aircraft is not only a unique challenge, but today, it's also almost a requirement for a scale competitor who wants to win the "big one." So many of the aircraft we model today, such as warbirds, jets and even homebuilt aircraft, actually have the unpainted aluminum surfaces, or skins. To receive maximum scores in competition, these skins must be reproduced accurately. Models that have been painted silver to simulate aluminum can't compete with models that have been skinned with a "metalized" product. There are several such products available, and each one requires a different technique to achieve the most authentic results. I usually use Coverite* Presto metallic covering and an aluminum detailing foil sold by Foley Mfg.*

As with any finishing job, the surfaces that will be coated must be prepared; the model should be glassed and primed. Surface defects will be visible through any of the foil coverings, and they'll be emphasized by the covering's mirror finish.

PRIMING

Priming the model is important to enhancing the final effect. I use K&B* two-part epoxy primer, which is easy to work with and to sand. It's white right out of the can, but it can be tinted with the various K&B paints. A small gap will always exist between each metalized panel; the secret is to tint your primer so that these small spaces enhance the model and provide depth to its surface. A medium-to-dark charcoal gray primer usually works best.

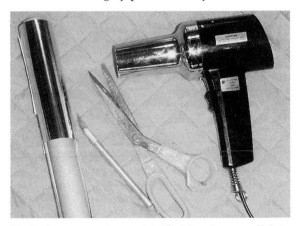

The tools necessary to complete the job: scissors, an X-Acto knife, a heat gun and covering material. The only items not pictured are the fine-line tape and the tack cloth.

WORKING WITH PRESTO

Applying the foil or aluminum panels is next. I like to start at the nose and work "radially" around the model toward the tail. When it's heated, Presto metallic covering will stretch, but it will *not* shrink. At this point, 3-views that show panel sizes and their locations are very helpful. Panels on full-scale aircraft are sized and shaped to perform certain functions; the extent to which aluminum skins can be formed is limited. I've found that scale panel sizes and shapes that are proportional to their full-scale counterparts can usually be applied without too much difficulty. When you try to do several panels with one piece of Presto, however, wrinkling and stretching become problems.
• If your fuselage does not already have molded-in panel lines, use a soft lead pencil to lay out the approximate panel locations. Mask the first panel's perimeter with ⅛-inch fine-line tape (available at automotive-supply stores).
• With scissors, cut the Presto approximately ½ inch larger than the desired panel shape.
• With a *good-quality* tack cloth, wipe your hands, the panel that's to be covered and both sides of the Presto panel.
• Carefully peel off its backing, and position the Presto.

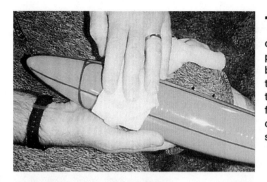

1 After the wing tank has been covered and the perimeter tape has been applied, the tack cloth is used to clean the surface to which the covering will be stuck.

2 Coverite Presto is applied to the wing tank. For this procedure, be sure to follow the directions in the text.

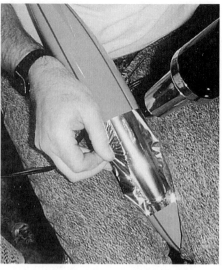

3 The author uses a heat gun to stretch the Presto over the model's surface. Presto will stretch when heat is applied, but it won't shrink.

• Starting along one edge, slowly press the Presto onto the model, gently sweeping your finger back and forth while you hold the other end of the Presto off the model. This method allows you to work all the air bubbles and wrinkles out as you move across the panel. If air or dirt becomes trapped under the Presto, just peel it off and start again.

• With your fingernail, crease the Presto down along the tape's edges, and use a sharp X-Acto blade and a flexible straightedge to trim it to meet the tape.

• Peel away the fine-line tape, and the panel is finished. Areas of separation, e.g., hatch openings and disk breaks, and compound curves require a different approach.

APPLYING THE PANEL

• **Fuselage.** I like to stick the panel down along the center of the fuselage and, using heat, slowly stretch the material out. When half of the panel has been applied, stretch the other half from the center out, and trim it to fit. If the surface curves are too severe, several smaller panels may be required. Over time, the Presto may peel away from panels that have exposed edges, such as those around hatch openings, gear doors and brakes. To avoid this problem, wipe these edges with a soft cloth that has been dampened with K&B thinner. Apply the Presto immediately after the thinner has dried.

Gaseous residue from the K&B thinner will actually "melt" the Presto adhesive onto the model. Any panels that have to be replaced will leave their adhesive behind. This residue can be removed with

K&B thinner before the new panel is applied. Continue this process, panel by panel, until your fuselage is complete.

• **Wings.** Wings are really no different to cover, but the panels are usually quite a bit larger. A slight change in the application method will help eliminate dirt and air bubbles on these large areas. After you've trimmed your Presto panel so that it's 1 inch larger all around than is necessary, peel *one* edge— *not the whole piece*—away from the backing. Stick this edge to the model, and while you work the Presto down with your fingers, gradually roll the backing off the panel as you apply it. With this method, large panels can be applied easily and with minimal waste.

BLENDING METAL AND PAINT

There are several schools of thought on how metallized panels can be blended into painted areas of the model. One possibility is to cover the entire model with Presto and then mask and paint the appropriate areas. I've also heard of modelers extending one panel of the Presto into the painted areas. To simulate panel seams, I use 1/64-inch drafting tape to mask and spray all the painted areas first. It's simple: apply the 1/64-inch tape around the panel perimeters, spray the model, and then peel off the tape. The remaining grooves look realistic, and they match up well with the Presto panels.

Then apply the Presto to all the open, non-painted areas of the model, and trim every panel

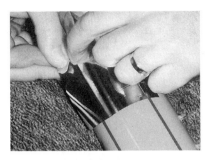

4 To define the lines needed for trimming around the covering's perimeter, use your fingernail to crease the Presto down along the tape edges.

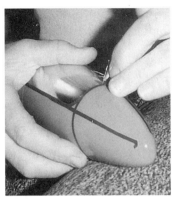

7 When you've finished trimming, peel off the fine-line tape, and you have a beautiful reproduction of an aluminum-skinned surface.

6 Carefully peel back the excess Presto, and continue the rest of the covering.

5 Use a sharp X-Acto knife and a flexible straightedge to trim away the excess Presto.

carefully along the masked edge. A good French-curve-style template cut out of thin plastic or flexible template material is helpful when you trim along painted edges.

REALISTIC DETAILS

• **Hatches and doors.** To simulate hatches, doors, etc., use Foley Mfg. 0.005-inch-thick aluminum detailing foil. It's adhesive-backed, and it's coated on the front to accept paint. To allow a natural aluminum finish, the coating can be removed with thinner.

Hatches, panels and various shapes can be cut out of this product and applied to the model's surface. Be very careful not to touch the adhesive on the back; fingerprints reduce its adhesiveness. Because it's slightly thicker than the surrounding material, this product produces effects that greatly enhance the model's appearance. To create hatches that share the same polished-aluminum look as the rest of the model, I put Presto over the Foley foil. Apply the Presto before you cut the panel to shape.

• **Rivets.** The most frequently asked question is probably, "How do you make those rivets look so realistic on scale models?"

Burning in rivets yields the most realistic results. Though it isn't a new idea, burning rivets into Presto requires a slightly different technique and heat-gun tip. The necessary tools for painted surfaces are typical: a small, pencil-type wood-burning tool, a rheostat to control temperature and a $\frac{1}{16}$-inch brass tube sharpened as shown in Figure A. For "riveting" Presto, the tip configuration must be shaped as shown in Figure B. To "rivet" paint, you want the tip to simultaneously burn and cut a small ring through the paint. To "rivet" Presto, you want to melt a donut shape into the plastic on the Presto's surface.

Temperature and pressure are critical. If the tool's tip is too hot, the plastic will "string out" as the tool is pulled away. With too much pressure, you'll burn a hole right through the Presto. The key is to practice on something else and perfect your technique before you "rivet" the model. I like the tip to be just warm enough to require minimal pressure. If the Presto starts to become stringy, simply blow on the tip to cool it just enough to continue.

• **Evenly spaced rivets.** The second most frequently asked question is how to maintain even spacing between rivets. I've tried using rulers, flexible straightedges and other measuring devices; they work OK, but after a while, the eyestrain becomes overwhelming, and you make mistakes. My biggest success was the result of using a very simple, 1-inch-wide, 6-inch-long, flexible template made of $\frac{1}{64}$-inch-thick plywood. To make it, draw a lengthwise centerline, and carefully mark and drill a series of $\frac{1}{16}$-inch holes on $\frac{3}{16}$-inch centers. Saw the strip almost in half (leave the centerline on the side to be used). You now have a simple, flexible, non-scratching template.

Position this template next to your panel seam,

and let the rivet tool nestle into each scallop in the wood; as you apply pressure, you produce a rivet—very simple and very effective.

For models that require raised rivets, aluminum powder can be mixed with Zap* Formula-560 glue. Use a glue gun or a syringe to place drops at each rivet location. Mike Barbee of Columbus, OH, has developed a neat technique for applying raised rivets. He dips the teeth from a curling-iron comb into the adhesive and presses the teeth against the model to produce about 20 perfectly spaced rivets at a time! It's a great time-saver.

GRAPHICS AND CLEARCOATING

For the graphics and clearcoating, I've used Aeroloft* dry transfers over metallic coverings with excellent results. For the best results, they should be applied after the rivets have been made. Burned-in rivets create an additional dimension in both paint and Presto. When a dry transfer has been placed over such a rivet and burnished down, the rivet shows through the transfer, and this produces a truly authentic look.

Before you apply any paint to the Presto covering, it's important to use a suitable bonding agent. There are two products on the market (available at automotive-supply stores) that work very well. Jerry Caudle has produced excellent results with Plastic Magic (no. 1050-4). I've used SEM's flexible Bumper Primer (no. 39864) with equally good results. Both products are clear, and a light coat is required before any top coating can be applied. I know of an instance where a standard bonding clear was used, and it didn't work.

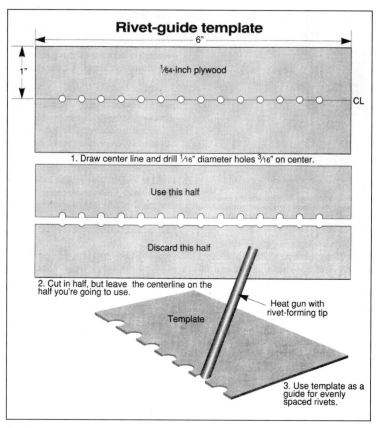

1. Draw center line and drill 1/16" diameter holes 3/16" on center.

Use this half

Discard this half

2. Cut in half, but leave the centerline on the half you're going to use.

Template

Heat gun with rivet-forming tip

3. Use template as a guide for evenly spaced rivets.

Outlines of the different tips needed to create rivets on covered surfaces and painted surfaces. Great care must be taken when making "rivets."

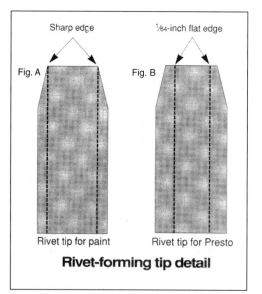

Sharp edge

1/64-inch flat edge

Fig. A

Fig. B

Rivet tip for paint

Rivet tip for Presto

Rivet-forming tip detail

burnish the surface without first applying any clearcoat at all.

Masking off various adjacent panels and burnishing them in directions 90 degrees apart adds a nice, grain effect and distinguishes each panel. To enhance weathering, apply pastel chalk with a coarse brush; charcoal gray and dark browns work best.

WEATHERING

For authenticity, the model's surface must be weathered. Presto is best suited to the highly polished aluminum look, but you can dull it by burnishing the surface with no. 000 steel wool. I like to do this after the clearcoat has been applied. If the dulling is overdone, some of the gloss can be restored with a high-grade polishing compound. In cases where more severe weathering is required,

This process is tedious and time-consuming, but the results are worth the effort. When your metallized model is at the field or a contest, and you're asked, "Wow! How did you get that realistic-looking metal finish?", you can be proud of yourself and your new-found skills.

Addresses are listed alphabetically in the Index of Manufacturers on page 146.

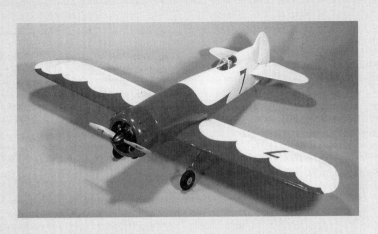

3

Working with foam, fiberglass and plastic

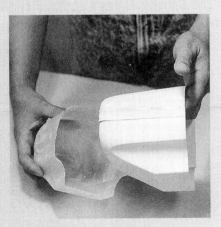

Sheet foam wings with plain brown paper
by Bertil Klintbom

You can create a perfect finish with brown wrapping paper. This method is easy, low-cost and creates a clean, strong surface that's very tough and resists punctures. If you like, you can cover an entire model this way! I covered the wing and parts of the fuselage of my ⅛-scale Casa 212 Aviocar this way.

1 Add leading and trailing edges and the wingtip to the foam-core. Mix regular white glue 50:50 with water and add some food coloring. Cut the brown wrapping paper so that the top sheet is 1 inch wider than the foam-core, and the bottom sheet is slightly smaller than the chord of the foam-core. If there is a "grain" to the paper, it should be positioned spanwise.

Apply the glue mixture to the foam-core; you can see why you need to color it!. Coat both sides of the foam-core and the matte side of the paper with the glue mixture.

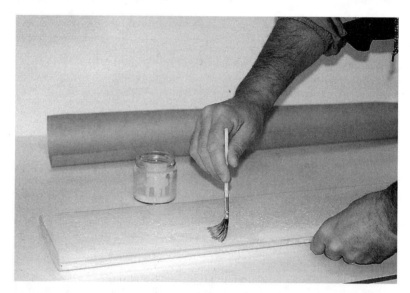

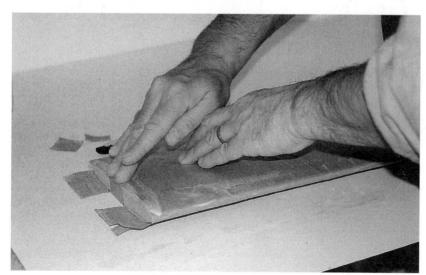

2 Position the paper on the foam-core. Start with the underside and continue with the upper surface. The upper sheet should overlap the edges and the bottom sheet. Smooth out the paper with your hands and work quickly, before the paper gets too wet. Make sure to cover both sides of the foam-core!

Cut the paper at the wingtip and root and fold small pieces of it up over the side to the bottom surface. If you have a rounded wingtip, simply cut darts in the paper and let the pieces overlap.

3 After you've covered the wing, it will start to wrinkle and look awful: a total disappointment! No problem; hang it to dry for 24 hours, and it will be smooth again.

4 After the wing has completely dried, coat it with a mixture of 50:50 water and white glue. The cover will wrinkle again, but hang it to dry, then repeat this process once more.

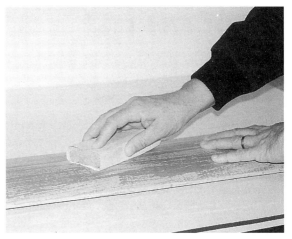

5 After the wing has completely dried for the third time, dry-sand it. Be careful not to cut into the paper surface.

6 Fill out the paper joints with lightweight filler, and after the wing has dried, sand the joints and add more filler if needed.

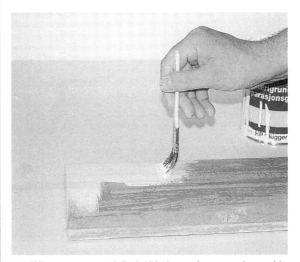

7 When you are satisfied with the surface, continue with a primer and paint as usual. If you wet-sand the wing, be sure you have a good coat of primer on the surface. ✦

Prepare foam and fiberglass for painting

by Bob Fiorenze

Some people get very nervous when they discover that a kit they're interested in has a fuselage made of fiberglass (whether polyester or epoxy), and the wing, stab and vertical fin are made of foam and balsa. They have never worked with this type of construction, and they are intimidated. Well, here are a few tips to help relieve the tension.

FIBERGLASS FUSE

First, determine whether the fuselage was damaged during shipping. If it was, and the damage is extensive, call the manufacturer for a replacement. If the damage is slight, you can fix it yourself, following this procedure:

• Cut a piece of ¾-ounce fiberglass cloth (I recommend K&B* lightweight cloth no. 8161) approximately ¼ inch wide and ½ inch longer than the break.

• Next, lightly sand the area around the damage with 220-grit sandpaper.

• Now, place the cloth patch directly over the damaged area (on the outside of the fuselage). With this method, cracks won't open or show through the paint (see photo 1).

• Using medium CA (Pacer Technology* PT-02), glue the cloth patch to the fuselage, and lightly sand again with 220-grit sandpaper.

• Fill and feather with the body putty of your choice. (I use Nitro Stan glaze putty, found at auto-supply stores.)

If there wasn't any damage, proceed this way:

• Remove the wax or mold-release agent from the fiberglass. (Prep Sol, an automotive wax remover,

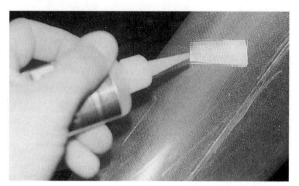

1 To repair a crack in the fiberglass, lightly sand the area. Then place the cloth patch directly over the damaged area (on the outside of the fuselage). Using medium CA, glue the cloth patch to the fuselage, and lightly sand with 220-grit sandpaper. With this method, the crack can never open or show through the paint.

works well for this.)

• Saturate a clean cloth, and wipe down the entire body; repeat with another clean rag or a paper towel. You don't want any wax residue on the fuselage, because the next step is to sand (preferably wet-sand) with 220-grit sandpaper. Wax residue can prevent paint from bonding tightly with the model's surface. This can cause problems with paint adhesion; the paint can lift off the surface if the model is left out in the sun at the flying field.

• Now is a good time to put on those bifocals to look for pinholes. Carl Goldberg's* Model Magic Filler no. 795 works well here, as does BVM* Pinhole Filler no. 1925. Generally, I use a sponge or a paper towel to rub the filler into the entire fuselage from all oblique angles to ensure that all the pesky little holes are filled. Now is not the time to

2 When preparing wood-covered foam wings, first sand with 220-grit sandpaper. Next, reinforce highly stressed areas, such as spar locations, servo cutouts, etc., with square patches of 2-ounce fiberglass cloth.

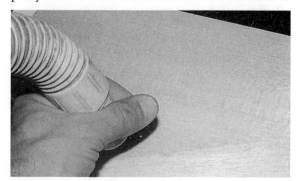

3 Remove all traces of balsa dust by vacuuming or wiping with a rag, being careful not to ding the balsa surfaces.

conserve filler; if you do, be prepared to repeat this step. When the filler is dry, lightly sand the entire fuselage again with 320-grit sandpaper. At this time, all the holes should be filled.

PRIMER POINTERS

It's time to prime. If you plan to prime with spray cans, use a product called Plasticote Sandable Primer, found at auto-supply stores. It's very important that the label says "sandable primer." Non-sandable primer will clog and "ball up" the sandpaper (grief and agony). If you have a compressor and spray equipment, you can make a 50:50 mix of primer and thinner. In either case, spray the entire fuselage heavily; it's OK for now. Allow the primer to dry, then sand the entire fuselage with 220- to 320-grit sandpaper, and sand most of the primer away. You'll know it's time to stop sanding when the only primer that remains is in the hairline cracks, low spots and sanding scratches (if any).

At this time, your fuselage will look like some kind of multicolored, patched-up mess. Do not despair; you are doing well. Wipe down and reprime the entire fuselage. Be cautious with how much primer you spray on (not too much this time), and let it dry. Don't do any more prep work until all construction on the model has been completed.

FOAM-CORE WINGS

Prepare wood-covered foam wings the same way as you would prepare for covering with MonoKote*:
• Sand first with 220-grit sandpaper (see photo 2).
• Next, reinforce highly stressed areas, such as spar locations, servo cutouts, etc., with square patches of 2-ounce fiberglass cloth (medium); use epoxy or polyester resins to apply the patches.
• Let them dry, then sand them with 220-grit sandpaper. Remove all traces of balsa dust by vacuuming or wiping with rags; be careful not to ding the balsa surfaces (photo 3).
• Cut ¾-ounce fiberglass cloth (photo 4) large enough to cover each wing panel. Apply polyester resin or epoxy (I recommend Pacer Technology Z-Poxy PT-40) to each wing panel with the cloth lying on its surface. Squeegee excess resin from the center out toward the edges of the wing panels. (You can make a squeegee out of an old playing card or 1/64-inch-thick plywood.)
• Let the wings dry, then lightly sand high spots with 220 sandpaper. When I say "lightly," I mean you shouldn't sand for longer than 20 seconds on each wing panel. Any longer than that, and you are working too hard. Sand off excess cloth around the perimeter with a scrap piece of 220-grit sandpaper (photo 5).
• Apply a second coat of resin and repeat the process. Spray primer onto the wings and stab as you did on

4 Cut pieces of ¾-ounce fiberglass cloth large enough for each wing panel. Apply polyester resin or epoxy to each wing panel with the cloth lying on the panel's surface.

5 Sand excess cloth off the perimeter with a scrap of 220-grit sandpaper. Apply a second coat of resin and repeat the process.

6 Here are the products used in this article (not including the Prep Sol and the Nitro Stan).

the fuselage, and sand between coats. Finally, sand with 400-grit sandpaper.

BEFORE YOU PAINT

When you are ready to paint, wipe the fuselage with Prep Sol again. Because you have been handling the aircraft, you may have deposited oil and grease on it, or there may be pencil reference marks or masking-tape residue. All these must be removed. (Photo 6 shows the products used in this article.)

As you can see, it takes a little time and patience to prepare fiberglass and foam/wood wings for painting. As you tackle your next painting project, don't be intimidated; just remember: "Make haste—slowly."

*Addresses are listed alphabetically in the Index of Manufacturers on page 146.   ◆

Mixing epoxy resin

by Chuck Anderson

I developed this balance about 15 years ago because, when I switched to epoxy resin for building fiberglass fuselages, I found that different products required different mixing ratios, and I needed a tool to generate the proper mixture of resin and hardener. This balance is easy to use, and I have found it to be at least as accurate as a lab-quality beam balance when mixing resin, especially when mixing very small amounts.

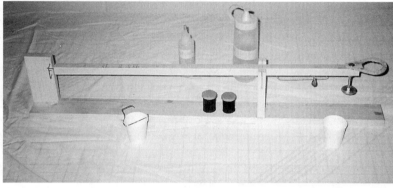

The balance is a single-cup system in which the balance is leveled with an empty resin cup in the holder and no weight on the zero position of the balance arm.

This balance was designed around the plastic cups sold for use with standard 3-ounce bathroom dispensers. I find this to be a convenient size since I seldom mix more than 2 ounces of resin at a time. Other cups may be used by changing the resin-cup holder as long as the dimension from the center of the cup to the pivot is not changed. Materials can be purchased at any home building supply store for less than $5. If you happen to have a well-stocked scrap box, you might even have enough scrap to build the balance. Only the balance beam weight cup, pivot and resin-cup locations shown in the drawing are critical. Other dimensions may be changed to fit available materials. The balance can be built smaller; the dimensions chosen were selected to maximize accuracy and simplify calculations for the weight cup locations for various resin-to-hardener ratios.

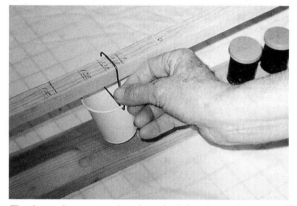

The beam is measured and marked for the various resin/hardener ratios to be mixed.

CONSTRUCTION

Begin by cutting a 36-inch-long base from 1x3-inch white wood. (Tip: check the wood in the "white wood" bin carefully. I have found good, straight-grained spruce in the white wood bin.) Also cut a 5-inch balance pivot support and a 5.5-inch pointer scale from the same wood. Cut a slot for the balance beam in the pivot support. Slot the pivot support for the utility blade using a razor saw or hacksaw blade. An easy way to be sure that the slot is parallel to the 3-inch face is to lay the pivot block on a flat surface and use ⅜-inch strips to guide the saw blade. Attach the pivot support and pointer guide to the base at the correct locations using nails and carpenter's glue.

Cut a 30-inch length of 1-inch-square wood for the balance beam. Lay out the cup holder on ⅛-inch plywood. Draw the centerline for the holes, and make sure that the lines cross the rim. Carefully cut out the hole for the resin cup,

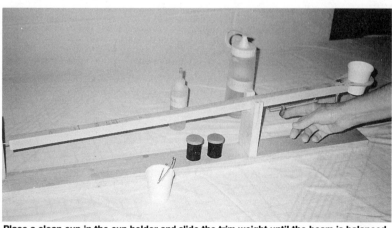

Place a clean cup in the cup holder and slide the trim weight until the beam is balanced.

and make sure that the hole is centered. Errors in the location of the hole for the resin cup will reduce the balance accuracy. When you're satisfied with the fit and location of the resin-cup hole, finish cutting out the cup holder, and glue it to one end of the balance beam using carpenter's glue.

When the glue has set, tape a scrap of cardboard over the bottom of the cup holder, and re-draw the centerline of the hole. Measure exactly 10 inches from the center of the cup holder, and carefully draw a line perpendicular to the beam. Use a square to transfer the location to the bottom of the beam, and cut a shallow notch for the pivot. The notch must be exactly 10 inches from the center of the resin cup and perpendicular to the beam, so take your time. Now lay out the weight cup positions for epoxy ratios of 5 to 1, 2.22 to 1 and 1 to 1 as shown in the plans.

The balance is now marked for the three most commonly used epoxies. If you need another ratio, the distance from the pivot point to the weight cup location for any ratio is simply the parts per 100 of hardener divided by 10 plus 10.

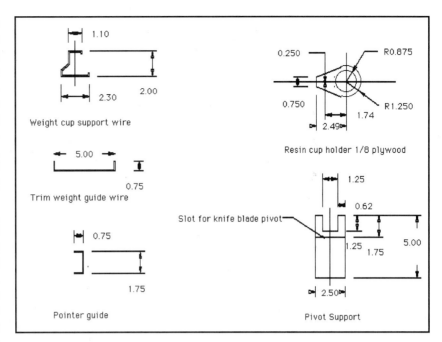

Distance = parts per 100/10 + 10

The calculation for E-Z Lam* is therefore

Distance = 45/10 + 10 = 14.5 inches

The reason for selecting 10 inches for the distance from the resin cup to the pivot is to simplify calculation of the distance measurements for any ratio.

When you calculate the distance, be sure to use parts per 100 when measured by weight. For example, the ratio for E-Z Lam is 45 parts per 100 when measured by weight or 50 parts per 100 when measured by volume. West System* epoxy is 20 parts per 100 (5 to 1) whether measured by weight or volume.

Drill a ¼-inch hole and install a 3-inch-long carriage bolt for the counterweight. The trim weight slide wire, weight cup holder and beam pointer stop are bent up from ¹⁄₁₆-inch soft iron wire. Drill a slightly undersize pilot hole for the trim weight slide wire. Slide a 1-ounce fishing sinker on the slide wire, and press into place. Drive a small finishing nail or scrap of wire into the end of the balance arm to serve as a pointer. Mark the location of the pointer on the pointer scale, and install the wire pointer guide. Punch holes

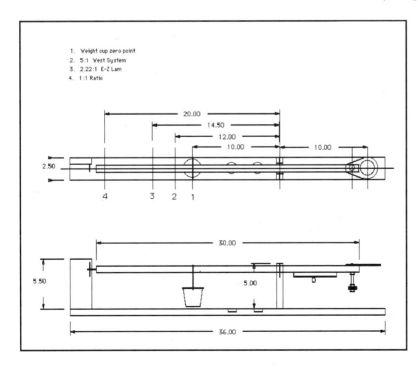

on each side of a 3-ounce cup, and slide it on the wire hanger.

Almost any weights can be used with this balance; I have found that 0.1-ounce lead sinkers are the easiest to use, while lead shot is useful if fine adjustments are needed. I keep these weights in 35mm film canisters. If you decide to use these, then drill two 1.25-inch-diameter holes halfway through the base between the pivot support and the zero weight location.

This is the time to paint the balance if you desire. Painting the balance will give a more professional look as well as make cleanup easier. I didn't bother with a finish and used the original balance for over 15 years. I did wipe the balance with acetone occasionally to remove uncured resin and had no problems.

The pivot is a blade from a utility knife epoxied into the slot on top of the pivot support. Be sure that the top edge of the blade is parallel with the base of the support. If all dimensions are accurate, then the dimensions shown in the drawing will be sufficient. Otherwise, you have to correct it by calibration. The balance adjustment weight compensates for slight variations in the weight of the resin cup and is a 1-ounce lead fishing sinker. Set the balance on a level surface, and install the balance arm. Slide the trim weight to the center of the wire, and add nuts and washers to the counterweight bolt until the beam balances with an empty 3-ounce paper cup in the resin-cup holder, no weight cup installed and the adjust weight centered. Any material can be used for the weight; large, flat washers clamped between two nuts are the easiest to handle. My original balance used a Cox glow head wrench left over from long-gone Cox engines. (I used to fly free-flight, too.)

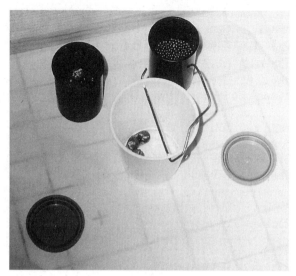

Add sufficient weight to the weight cup for the amount of resin you want to mix. Small, 0.1-ounce lead sinkers make handy weights.

CALIBRATION

If the dimensions of the balance arm are accurate, then the dimensions shown should be good enough for mixing resin. If errors are found in any of the dimensions, then the scale will have to be corrected. In any event, a calibration check should be performed to verify the scales.

You need a roll of new pennies to calibrate the balance. Remove the weight cup, install an empty 3-ounce cup in the resin-cup holder, and adjust the trim weight until the pointer on the balance beam is aligned with the mark on the pointer scale. Place 20 pennies in the resin cup, and make sure that the pennies are evenly distributed in the bottom of the cup. Hang the weight cup on the zero line of the balance beam, and add water to the weight cup until the beam again balances. Then add four pennies to the resin cup, and move the weight cup until the beam balances. The cup should be on the 5:1 line. If the location of the weight cup is off more than $\frac{1}{32}$ inch, erase the 5:1 mark and redraw it at the weight cup location. This is the location for West System epoxy. Add five more pennies to the epoxy cup, and repeat the check for 2.22:1 location. This is the location for E-Z Lam epoxy. Now add 11 pennies to the epoxy cup, and repeat the check for the 1:1 location.

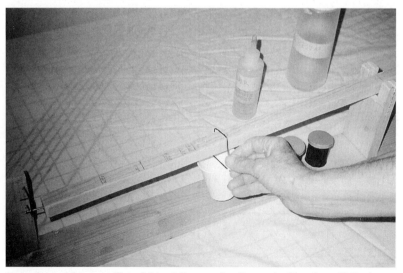

Hang the weight cup with weights at the zero location and add resin until the beam balances.

MIXING RESIN

Measuring resin could be done just like the calibration; however, it is easier to hang the desired weight at the zero location and then add resin until the beam is balanced. Almost anything can be used for weights; 0.1-ounce split lead sinkers make very good weights and are easy to use. The weight cup and wire also should weigh about 0.1 ounce, so if you need 1 ounce of resin, all you have to do is place nine sinkers in the weight cup.

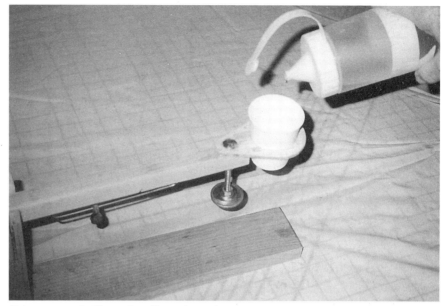

Using squeeze bottles makes dispensing resin easy.

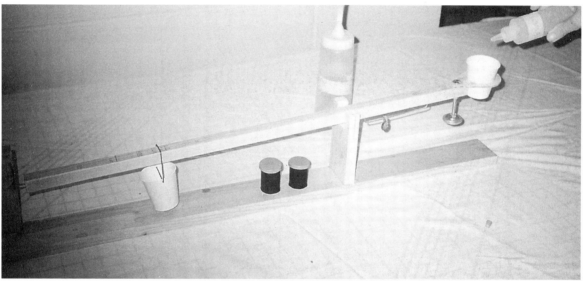

Move the weight cup to the proper ratio mark and add hardener until the beam balances.

Place a clean cup in the resin-cup holder, and slide the trim weight until the beam is balanced. Then hang the weight cup with weights on the balance beam at the zero location. Now carefully add resin until the beam balances. A squeeze bottle like those used by E-Z Lam makes it easier to control the amount of resin and hardener being added to the resin cup. Relaxing the pressure on the bottle stops the flow of resin or hardener instantly. If an excessive amount of resin is added to the cup, add weight to the weight cup until the beam balances. Lead shot is good for making fine adjustments to the weight in the cup but shouldn't be needed if you are careful.

Move the weight pan to the desired ratio point, and carefully add hardener to the resin cup until the beam is balanced. Be especially careful when you add hardener since it is not possible to accurately add the correct amount of resin if you get too much hardener.

I have been using this type of balance for mixing epoxy resins for over 15 years and have found that it gives me the most accurate mixes, and this makes the job of mixing epoxies much more rewarding.

Addresses are listed alphabetically in the Index of Manufacturers on page 146. ♦

Make your own fiberglass cowls

by Brian Bange

When the ABS cowl on my airplane cracked, I decided that a fiberglass replacement cowl would be a good alternative. Unfortunately, I found that fiberglass cowls could be a bit costly, and they aren't available for some models. At this point, I realized that I could make my own using a kit-supplied ABS cowl as a mold.

Read on as I describe the process and the materials you'll need, which are mostly inexpensive. The West System* epoxy is not, but I've found that 1 quart will go a long way. I made five molds, six cowls and two wheel pants, and I skinned the front half of my Ultimate, and I still have ⅓ quart left. It's first-class. Overnight, it cures so hard that a part may be removed from the mold in the morning and sanded, and it doesn't plug the sandpaper.

MATERIALS

These materials work well for me and are the minimum I recommend for a successful job.

- 1 quart West System no. 105 epoxy resin
- Hardener—West System no. 206 (25-minute pot life), or 209 (45-minute pot life). Note: the lower the temperature, the longer the cure time.
- 1 yard 3.16-ounce satin-weave fiberglass cloth
- 1 yard 6-ounce loose-weave fiberglass cloth
- Disposable plastic gloves
- Paste wax (no silicone!)
- Wax paper
- A flexible, flat-bottom container, e.g., an empty butter tub
- Flux brushes (usually 15 to 20 cents at your local hardware store)
- Stirring stick

1 Wax your ABS part with plenty of non-silicone wax; I use Partall* paste no. 2. Make sure that there isn't any silicone in your wax; if silicone gets onto your part, you'll never be able to make paint stick to it.

2 Cut out square pieces of both thicknesses of glass cloth. The size that works best for me measures about 3 inches square. If the cowl has small features such as scoops, cut small pieces of the 3.16-ounce cloth to fit into them. Cut enough cloth to cover the entire ABS cowl once with the 3.16-ounce cloth and twice with the 6-ounce cloth.

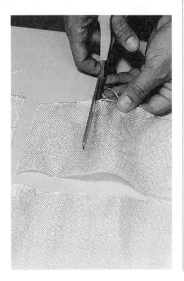

3 Mix 2 ounces of epoxy resin and the appropriate amount of hardener in a large plastic tub. Try to use a container that has a large flat bottom. The shallower the epoxy, the longer its pot life. West System sells epoxy pumps that meter the right amounts of epoxy and hardener. They last for several cans and really take the guesswork out of mixing.

4 Put on your disposable plastic gloves and place the ABS cowl nose-up on a piece of wax paper. Put the squares of 3.16-ounce cloth onto the outside of the cowl. Paint the resin over the cloth; it will seep through and stick to the ABS. The weave of the cloth is very loose, and it will conform to the contour of the cowl. I haven't had problems with wrinkles.

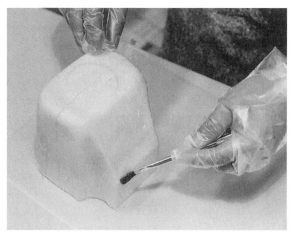

5 When the cowl is completely covered with 3.16-ounce cloth, immediately switch to the 6-ounce cloth and paint on two more layers. When you've finished, let it cure for 12 hours; longer, if your shop is cold.

6 When you return, the epoxy should be rock-hard, yet the entire mold will be slightly flexible. The ragged edge of the cloth is sharp and will cut like a knife, so use a Dremel tool or a sanding disk to remove any sharp

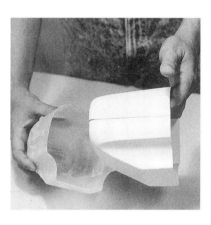

edges. After that, flex the mold gently and watch as the fiberglass comes off the ABS (you'll be able to see this through the epoxy). The area that has separated from the fiberglass will look lighter. By gently squeezing and twisting the mold, try to remove the entire ABS part without damaging it. If you used plenty of wax in step 1, it will pay dividends here. You now have a female mold of your cowl. With it, you'll be able to make many copies of the original ABS cowl.

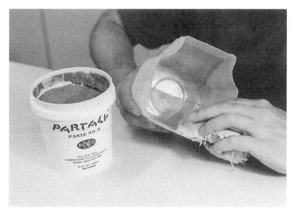

7 Wax the inside of the fiberglass mold as you did in step 1.

8 Cut more squares of fiberglass, as you did in step 2. Mix 2 ounces of epoxy, and paint the squares onto the mold as you did in steps 4 and 5. In areas that will be subjected to high stress, add more layers of cloth. Try to keep the epoxy layers as thin as possible; the cloth will change color as it's wetted, and using more epoxy than you need to wet it will add only weight, not strength. When you've finished, let the part cure for 12 hours.

9 Now for the fun. As in step 6, squeeze and twist the mold to separate it from the cowl. After some coaxing, it will pop out, and you'll be rewarded with a perfect copy of your ABS

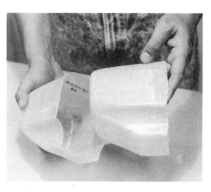

cowl. Cut openings for your engine and exhaust system, then finish-sand it and paint it with a thin coat of primer. If there are any pinholes or bubbles, they'll become visible. Fill them, sand once more, and you'll be ready for your finish color.

Although this process takes two days, the actual work time is usually less than 2 hours for the first part and less than 1 hour for every additional part. (Remember to re-wax the mold between parts.)

Note: if it's to be successfully removed from the mold, the ABS part must have "draw angle," i.e., as the part sits on the bench with the spinner side facing upward, nowhere should there be an angle between the part and the bench that's greater than 90 degrees. An angle of less than 90 degrees is preferable and will make removing the part easy. Most ABS cowls are vacuum-formed over a plug, so they always have a proper draw angle.

If you have flying buddies with similar planes to yours, you might be able to convince them to buy one of your cowls, and that will help to offset the cost of your materials. At my club, Lanier Stingers are popular, and several sport fiberglass cowls have been made with my mold.

I find making my own parts in this way very rewarding, and I'm already dreaming up ways to make other parts using this process. I hope you'll try it.

Make easy cowl mounts

by Gerry Yarrish

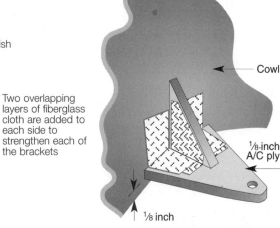

Two overlapping layers of fiberglass cloth are added to each side to strengthen each of the brackets

Cowl

⅛-inch A/C ply

⅛ inch

One of the most annoying problems modelers have to deal with when attaching a radial cowl is that, sooner or later, the external mounting screws wear and eventually crack the screw holes. The visibility of the screw heads also presents a cosmetic problem. Here's an easy way to eliminate these problems and simplify cowl attachment.

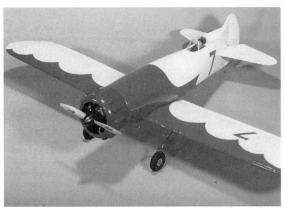

When I began my project—the Gentle Gee Bee (*Model Airplane News* plan FSP12941)—I already had a cowl waiting for a suitable airframe to be built behind it. The plans didn't show how to install the cowl, so I devised my own simple solution. You can adapt this method to other models that require a radial cowl.

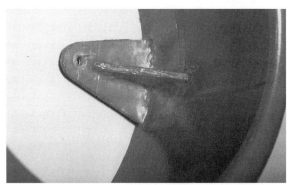

The secret lies within! These simple plywood mounting brackets allow the finished cowl to be screwed directly to the firewall's face. I used ⅛-inch-thick AC plywood to form the "T" cross-section bracket, and I glued the two pieces that make up each bracket with thick Balsa USA* Gold CA. For a super-strong bond to the plastic cowl, I applied two overlapping layers of fiberglass cloth. The glass is applied with thin CA and "kicked" with accelerator. When they've been glued into position, the brackets are sealed to fuelproof the wood grain. For an 8-inch-diameter cowl, I've found that four brackets set 90 degrees apart work well. A smaller cowl could use three brackets, and a giant-scale cowl could use six, eight, or even 10 brackets.

Here's the radial cowl that I used on my Henry Haffke-designed, sort-a-scale Gee Bee. Notice the clean appearance—no visible attachment screws to spoil its lines. Scratch-built from *Model Airplane News* plans, the Gee Bee uses a plastic, ⅙-scale, Pica* Waco biplane cowl.

Here you see how easy it is to install the cowl. I simply screw it into place using Du-Bro* socket-head screws. To reach the screws through the open front of the cowl, you'll need a long ball-end Allen wrench. There's plenty of space for the brackets to clear items such as the muffler, the engine, the throttle linkage, etc. Because the long Allen wrench can easily reach between the cylinder heads, this system could also be used even if you have a dummy radial engine in the front of the cowl.

Addresses are listed alphabetically in the Index of Manufacturers on page 146.

Make fiberglass wheel covers

by John Tanzer

I needed 7-inch, disk-type wheels for a giant-scale biplane I'm building, and I decided that the easiest solution would be to add fiberglass disk wheel covers to some commercially available wheels. I ordered a set of Sullivan Products* 7-inch wheels. These well-made, good-looking wheels have firm rubber tires with the words "AIRFLIGHT CUSTOM, ARAMID BELTED, INFLATE TO 30PSI MAX" in raised letters on the sidewalls. The two-piece aluminum hub is held together with six socket-head screws and locknuts, and the center bushing is nylon and is bored out for a ¼-inch axle. The wheels weigh 15 ounces each.

For the fiberglass mold, use an aluminum pot lid with the proper curve and with its center knob removed. Cover it with clear heat-shrink plastic pulled tight and taped to the back, then heat-shrink the front. Cut three disks out of 6-ounce fiberglass cloth. Lay these on the plastic, alternating the weave direction so the part will be stiff. Mix up some Z-Poxy* finishing resin, which wets out the cloth well and makes a rigid but flexible part. When mixing resin, always measure an exact 50:50 mix. When it has been thoroughly mixed, pour resin onto the cloth and spread it with a brush.

Before

After

Before and after. What a difference!

After the cloth has been completely wetted, cover it with another piece of heat-shrink plastic. Pull it tight and tape it at the back, then shrink it with the heat gun. (If you don't use enough resin, and pinholes develop later, you can fill them with spackle.) Let the resin cure overnight, then remove the top layer of plastic. Using a compass with a Magic Marker taped to it, mark a 4¼-inch circle, remove the part from the mold and cut the disk out with

PHOTOS BY JOHN TANZER

1. Sullivan Products 7-inch AirFlight wheels. These well-made, good-looking wheels weigh 15 ounces each.

2. The materials needed to make a disk-type wheel: a commercially available wheel, 6-ounce fiberglass, Z-Poxy, clear heat-shrink plastic and an aluminum pot lid with its center knob removed.

3. The clear heat-shrink plastic has been shrunk tight. We're ready for glass cloth.

4. Z-Poxy resin is applied to the glass cloth.

5. Top piece of clear heat-shrink plastic taped and shrunk over the wet glass cloth.

6. After the resin has cured, remove the top plastic.

7. Draw a circle on the fiberglass using a Magic Marker taped to a compass.

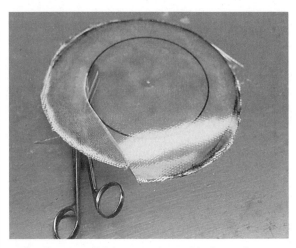

8. The fiberglass disk is cut to shape with sharp scissors.

9. "X" marks the spot where the disk screw hole lines up with the dowel.

10. The finished wheel cover parts and wheel with parts installed.

11. Same treatment using C.B. Tatone wheels. Note the plywood ring used as the cover mount.

sharp scissors. Leave the plastic on the mold to make the second disk.

The inner wheel disk is flat and made of fiberglass flat stock, phenolic sheet, aluminum or 1/32-inch plywood. Fiberglass flat stock can be made by sandwiching three pieces of 6-ounce cloth between two pieces of 1/2-inch plywood covered with heat-shrink plastic. To mark the inner flat disk for 3/8-inch dowels, hold the disk against the back of the wheel and use a pencil to mark dowel locations through the holes in the wheel hub. Cut six 3/8-inch dowels for each wheel, and screw them into the inner disk. Use Zap* CA to glue the dowels to prevent them from turning. To install the front disk, push the inner disk with dowels through the wheel, then lay the outer disk on the dowels. The disk is transparent and is easily drilled for no. 2 button-head screws. Mark one dowel and screw hole on the

inside of the disk with an "X." This will aid in assembly later.

Glue a ring washer to the center of the outer disk for a scale look, then prime and paint the disks. To mount a wheel on an axle, install an inner 1/4-inch wheel collar, then put the inner disk with dowels through holes in the wheel hub, and slide the wheel on with an outer 1/4-inch wheel collar to retain it. Now you can mount the outer wheel cover using the "X" to position the screw holes in the dowels. I've added fiberglass disks to C.B. Tatone* wheels as well. I glued plywood rings to the inner and outer wheel rims so that I would have something to attach the disks to.

Try this method. It works well for me.

*Addresses are listed alphabetically in the Index of Manufacturers on page 146.

Make fiberglass wheel pants

by Chris Batcheller

S imply put, adding wheel pants to your model is like putting icing on a cake. They're aerodynamic, add scale realism and just plain look good. It couldn't be easier to make fiberglass wheel pants to your exact specifications. Here's how.

PHOTOS BY CHRIS BATCHELLER

1 You'll need spray adhesive, wax paper, sharp scissors, an old hobby knife with a sharp blade, latex gloves, fiberglass resin and hardener (Bondo brand is easy to mix and is available at auto-parts stores), fiberglass cloth, a paint brush, a tongue depressor, a plastic squeegee and a mixing tub. You'll also need white glue, 150-grit sandpaper, a sanding block, an electric sander, a Dremel tool with a cutoff wheel and blue foam.

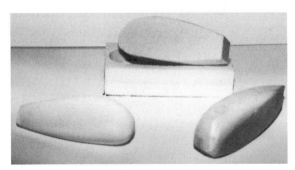

2 If you bought 1- or ¾-inch-thick foam, spray a light coat of adhesive on each piece, let them sit for five minutes and then join the two pieces together. Cut the wheel-pant shapes out of the foam with a band saw and roughly sand the foam into the desired shape with a palm sander (Black and Decker's Quick Finish sander works great) using 150-grit paper. Final-sand with a soft sanding block. Any imperfections will be multiplied as you add layers of glass cloth, so sand carefully!

3 After you've finished sanding, seal the foam with two or three coats of white glue. Don't thin the glue down, as this will make the mixture bead up on the foam.

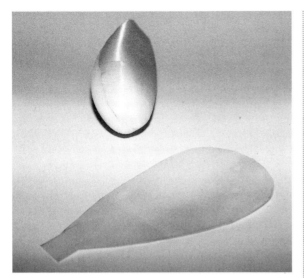

4 Prepare the fiberglass by laying it down on top of a brown paper bag. Apply spray adhesive over the fiberglass, then lay a sheet of wax paper on top of the fiberglass. Let this sit for approximately 10 minutes. Peel the fiberglass off the brown paper bag. You now have self-adhesive fiberglass with edges that won't fray. Cut a piece that's big enough so that the glass will wrap around the curves of the foam mold. Position the fiberglass on the foam and begin to work out all the wrinkles.

6 Spray a base coat of enamel paint on the wheel pants. Again, the hobby knife comes in handy while painting to keep the process hands-free. Be sure to spray several light coats; one heavy coat will run and won't produce good results.

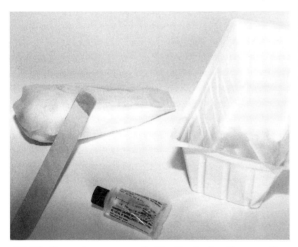

5 Mix the resin as suggested by the instructions on the bottle. Work quickly; use the tongue depressor to get the resin onto the wheel pant. When the fiberglass is saturated with resin, smooth out the glass with your fingers (make sure you have the gloves on!). To do this more easily, put a hobby knife in a vise with the blade up and place the wheel pant on the knife where the wheel opening will be. This way, you don't have to hold the pant while you smooth out the glass. Apply a layer of fiberglass to the other side of the mold and continue until you've applied four or five layers. Allow the resin to cure.

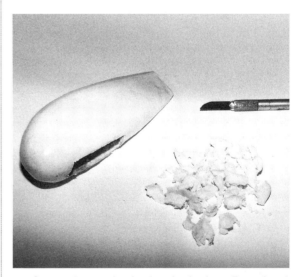

7 Cut out the opening for the wheel using a Dremel tool with a cutoff wheel. Dig the foam out from the inside of the wheel pant. Mount the pants on your airplane using commercially available hardware. Fun flying and happy landings! ✦

Cover fiberglass with MonoKote

by Faye Stilley

A fiberglass model airplane part doesn't have to be painted. I've heard horror stories about fellows spending $40 a quart to have paint mixed using a spectrum analyzer and still not getting an exact match to their film covering. You can be sure that your fiberglass parts will match the rest of the airplane only if you cover them with the same film; any graphics on the part will also match the airplane's trim-color scheme. The techniques used to cover fiberglass are only slightly different from those used to cover wood.

1 Preparing fiberglass for film covering is similar to preparing it for painting. First wash the parts thoroughly with soap and water to remove any release-agent residue. This is an important step. Then prime the part with finishing resin instead of with a paint primer. I've used Sig* polyester resin and Pacer* Z-Poxy finishing resin with equally good results. Depending on the quality of the fiberglass part, it will take from one to four coats, sanding between coats, to achieve a smooth finish. The objective is to get a satin finish, fill any pinholes and make the coating thick enough to prevent the weave of the fiberglass from showing through the film. Not all epoxy resins and polyester resins are compatible.

PHOTOS BY FAYE STILLEY

Before proceeding with the whole project, it is a good idea to do a small test on the inside of the part. If the resins aren't compatible, the coating simply won't cure; it won't damage the part. The wheel pant in the foreground has been sanded and is ready for covering. Even though you can see the weave in the glass, you cannot feel it. I used 220-grit sandpaper to smooth the surface and 400-grit sandpaper to polish it to a satin finish. The other pant has been coated with resin but not sanded. Resins cure to a high-gloss finish and are easy to sand.

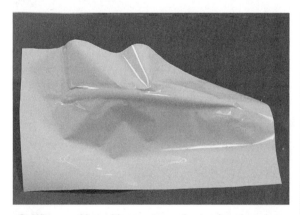

2 When working with a compound curved surface, iron the film onto the highest point of the curve first. Once attached from end to end, the film can be heated and stretched around the milder curves. A small covering iron with a rounded shoe works best for this; with the iron set at 220 to 230 degrees Fahrenheit, work fore and aft in "rows" of about ⅛ inch to 3/16 inch width. On each pass, heat the film until it becomes rubbery, stretch it until it conforms to the part's shape, then press it down onto the surface. Let the heat do the work; very little pressure is required.

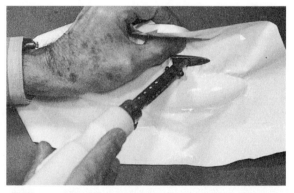

3 As you make your way away from the high point and down the side of the more mildly curved surface, make broader passes, perhaps ¼ inch to ⅜ inch wide. Lay the shoe of the iron on its side and use the "sole" to heat the film before it is stretched; then stretch it and slightly apply pressure with the side of the shoe. Note the position of the iron. I am heating the film in the area that will next be stretched into place. After pressing the film onto the surface, hold it in place. It needs to cool for the adhesive to attach firmly. Fiberglass does not dissipate heat as quickly as wood, so be prepared to hold the film in place for 3 to 5 seconds.

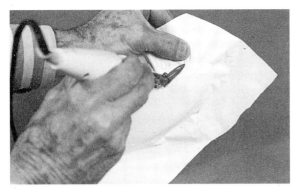

4 Here, the side of the pant is finished, and I am beginning to stretch the film around to the underside. The curve is quite sharp, and the bottom of the pant is nearly flat. In this situation, more heat needs to be applied, and more pull will be required to stretch the film around the curve. I have switched to a flat shoe on the iron and increased the temperature to the 260- to 280-degree range. The flat shoe works best because you can use just its tip to make narrow, 1/16-inch to 3/32-inch passes fore and aft. Sharp curves take a little more time than nice, big, round ones.

5 Here, one side of the pant is nearly complete. The covering extends just past the centerline along the top and bottom of the pant. To cover the top of the pant, I used the small rounded shoe, using the same technique as I used on the side. I was able to make fore and aft passes a little more than 1/4 inch wide from the high point to the centerline.

6 Draw a centerline, end to end, on the top and bottom of the pant. A small metal measuring tape makes the task easy; mine is on a key chain and is only 3/16 inch wide. Mark the center at the forward and aft ends of the pant. With masking tape, anchor the measuring tape on one end. While holding the tape in place, draw the centerline using a fine-line permanent marker. Cut the excess film away 1/32 inch beyond the centerline. The final seam will be only 1/16 inch wide and hardly noticeable.

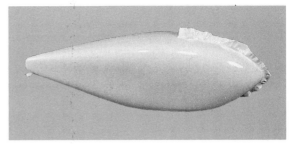

7 The reverse side of the pant is near completion and has been partly trimmed. If you look closely, you'll see that the top seam overlap is hardly visible. When approaching the seam area with film on the second side, be particularly careful not to seal it to the film that is in place. Stop short about 1/16 inch away. Use alcohol to remove the centerline you drew previously. Carefully ease the film up to, but not over, the film that's in place. Once again, with the small measuring tape, draw a line fore and aft. This time, draw a "cut line" rather than a centerline. This is the line you will follow to remove the excess material. Using the metal tape as a guide, draw a new, no. 11 X-Acto blade over the film. The object is to cut through the top layer of film without cutting the underlying film. It will take more than one pass with the knife. On the first pass, you will gently scribe the line without cutting through the film. Then you remove the measuring tape, and the scribe line will guide the blade on subsequent passes. You will find that you can cut through the film without cutting through the adhesive layer underneath; then just pull the excess film away.

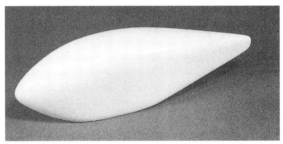

8 Here, the excess material has been removed and the seam has been sealed with heat. The cut line has been washed off with alcohol, and the pant is ready to be decorated with whatever graphics you choose. Not only does the pant exactly match the color of the airplane, but any graphics will be an exact match as well. As a bonus, your graphics will cost nothing because you can probably make them all from scrap covering material. You won't have to spend your whole allowance at the automotive paint store after all.

Addresses are listed alphabetically in the Index of Manufacturers on page 146. ✦

Heat-shrink plastic parts

by Randy Randolph

Vacuum-forming has been the method of choice used by most modelers to form plastic parts for their projects; unfortunately, it's a process that requires equipment not usually found in a modeler's workshop. Vern Williams of Little Rock, AR, offers this simple method for forming plastic parts that's almost like magic! Actually, it's better than magic, because it can be used to form cowls, cockpit canopies, windshields, cabin enclosures, hatch covers, or almost any part that will fit inside a plastic soft-drink bottle. The photos show the way.

1 The hardest part of the process is making a form for the part. When you make the form, allow for the thickness of the plastic and leave a little trim room all around. The form can be made of balsa, hardwood, plaster of Paris, or what have you. There must be a ¼-inch hole in the form's center in which a 12-inch-long dowel can be inserted to use as a handle. The form shown will make a cowl for a Mister Mulligan.

2 Cut the bottom off the bottle, insert the form, and snug it down against the neck of the bottle so that the dowel handle sticks out of the mouth. A two-liter bottle is shown, but the size of the form should dictate the size of the bottle. A clearance of ½ to ¾ inch between the part and the bottle is about right.

PHOTOS BY RANDY RANDOLPH

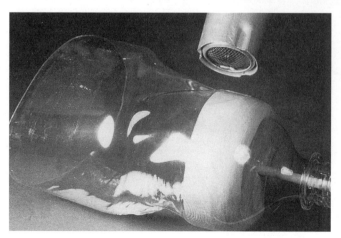

3 Start to form the part by applying heat from a heat gun to the section of the form that's away from the neck of the bottle. The heat will shrink the bottle down against the form; this will prevent the form from slipping out of the bottle. Work around the form, and shrink the bottle down against the sides of the form while you turn the bottle with the dowel handle.

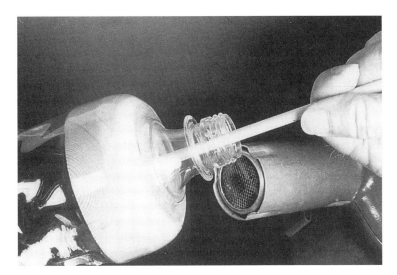

4 Move the heat gun to the neck end of the form, and shrink the bottle against the bottom of the form. Again, turn the bottle with the handle. The shrinking takes very little time—less than a minute.

5 Trim the bottle away from the widest part of the form, and use the dowel handle to push the form out of the part. After the form has been removed, the part can be trimmed to final shape. Oddly shaped parts can be formed in the same way using blocks of wood to take up the extra space in the bottle.

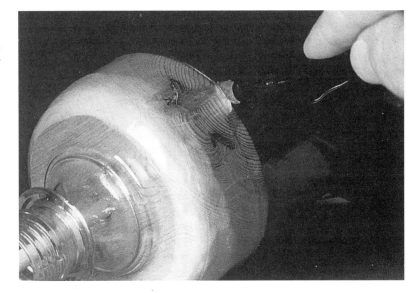

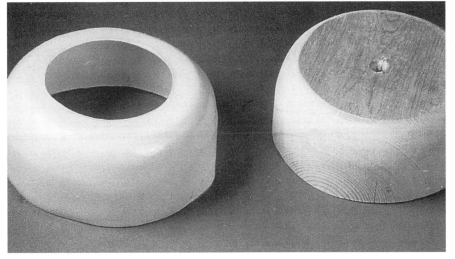

6 The finished part will show all the defects of the form, so a nice, smooth finish on the form works best. The formed parts can be painted on the inside for that perfect "deep" finish.

Make a vacuum-forming box

by Jim Sandquist

After getting past the trainer stage, many modelers want to build an airplane that looks more true-to-scale. All too often, however, many of the scale details on such kit models aren't provided by their manufacturer, but are left to the modeler's ingenuity. Having run into this problem a number of times for such things as air scoops, navigation lights, headsets for the pilot, etc., we decided to make a small vacuum-forming box to reproduce them. The photographs show you how.

• **Make a mold.** First, you have to make a male

mold of the part you want to duplicate. A mold can be made of balsa, hardwood, or foam. The mold doesn't have to be perfect, and there's no need to fill the wood grain. When the plastic is pulled over the mold, any imperfections will be on the inside; the outside of the finished part will be smooth.

When making taller pieces, it can be difficult for the vacuum to pull the plastic completely down over the mold. When this is the case, drill a few small holes in the mold to allow the air to be pulled through. Generally, I find that the molds take less than half an hour to make.

1 You'll need: Deluxe Project Case, RadioShack—part no. 270-223; pre-punched Perfboard; RadioShack—no. 276-1396; ¼-inch-thick plywood; heat gun; shop vacuum.

2 Cut the middle out of the Project Case lid. Cut a piece of the Perfboard to fit on the top of the open box lid. Cut a hole in the side of the case to accept your vacuum hose. This is what your parts should look like when they've been cut and are ready to be assembled. Make the box airtight by gluing the box lid and Perfboard to it with CA.

3 Make an 8x5-inch frame out of the ¼-inch-thick plywood to fit over the box.

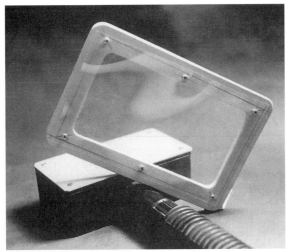

4 Screw a sheet of 20- or 30-gauge plastic to the plywood frame, and you're ready to vacuum-form a part.

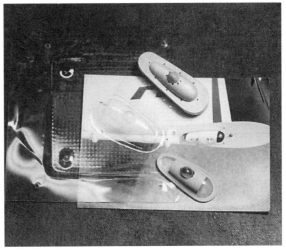

7 This shows navigation lights being formed; there's a completed part and one light primed and ready to be painted and detailed.

5 Put your mold on top of the box and, using a heat gun, heat the plastic until you see it start to sag a little. This will take only a few seconds.

• **Final steps.** After you have vacuum-formed the part, pop out the mold, trim away the excess plastic and paint it! This simple system will allow you to make parts of up to 5x3 inches in size. This is more than adequate for navigation lights, instrument panels, pilot accessories, air scoops and some small wheel pants and canopies.

Built for about $10, you will find this vacuum-forming system can really allow you to add some pizzazz to your planes, without extra weight or cost! ✦

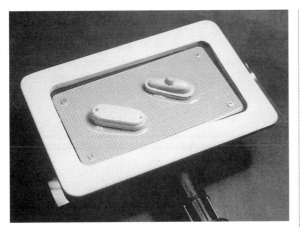

6 Then turn on your vacuum, lay the frame over the box and watch the plastic "pull down" instantly!

Easy vacuum-forming

by Syd Kelland

PHOTOS BY SYD KELLAND

Vacuum-forming your own canopies, wingtips, cowls and wheel pants is easier than you might think. Here are some of the secrets that will help you through the process and keep trial and error to a minimum.

I use a wooden vacuum box, my shop vac, a gas barbecue grill, the piece to be molded (called a plug) and some 20-gauge (ga) sheet plastic stapled to a plywood frame. I use the gas grill to heat the plastic because I like to work outside, but a kitchen oven will work just as well. I'm overly cautious when it comes to potentially harmful vapors that may be released when heating plastic.

THE VACUUM BOX

My airtight, 16x18-inch vacuum box is made of 1x4-inch lumber for the sides and ¼-inch-thick plywood for the top and bottom. In the top plywood piece, I drilled a pattern of ⅛-inch-diameter holes roughly ½ inch apart, radiating outward from the center point, and then I joined them with ¹⁄₁₆-inch-deep grooves made with my Dremel* tool and a cutoff wheel. I then glued a section of plastic pipe that accepts the hose from my shop vac into a hole on the side of the box. This is where the vacuum comes from.

On top of the box, around its perimeter, I added ½-inch foam weather-stripping tape, which will ensure a good, airtight seal over the entire working surface when I lay the hot plastic on top. Using my ordinary shop vac, I have been able to draw hot plastic down over a 3-inch plug without difficulty.

THE PLUG

Plugs can be made out of almost any material that you like to carve, as long as it can hold its shape under heat and moderate pressure. I carve plugs out of soft wood and then sand them down to the shape I want. I also like to use auto-body filler to add detail and build up any areas on the plug that need extra attention; the putty sets up quickly, is easily shaped with a rasp and can be sanded to a nice, smooth finish. If you make a plug out of foam, you will have to cover it with at least ¼ inch of plaster or body filler to protect it from the hot plastic.

Coat the plug with a thin oil film, which will work as a release agent. Do not use wax as a mold-release agent because the wax will stick to your plug like glue; trust me on this.

THE PLASTIC

Check the "Yellow Pages" for a local plastics supplier; you'll need 20ga styrene sheets (the least expen-

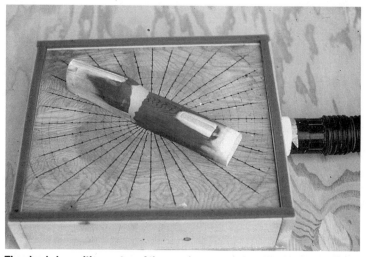

The plug is in position on top of the wooden vacuum box. The shop vac is connected through a hole on its side, and the weather-stripping ensures a good, airtight seal. Note the pattern of holes drilled in the top of the 16x18-inch vacuum box.

sive and easiest to work with), calendar vinyl and PET-G, ABS, TXP, or any other material suitable for thermal forming. Sheets typically measure 3x6 feet and cost $5 to $20 each, depending on the type of material. Styrene is white, and PET-G and TXP are clear and more suitable for canopies. (This is the kind of rigid, plastic sheet you see formed around consumer electronics products.)

I rough-cut the plastic sheet to the same size as the top of the vacuum box. By doing this, I ensure that there is a good, airtight seal between the hot plastic sheet and the weather-stripping around the vacuum box.

The plastic "sandwich" on the upper rack of the gas grill. The sheet metal on the grill ensures a more even heat distribution. I used a staple gun to secure the clear plastic sheet to the plywood frame.

FIRE UP THE BARBECUE

To vacuum-form successfully, it's important to heat your sheet plastic as evenly and as thoroughly as possible. To achieve an even heat distribution on my gas grill, I cover the entire area just above the fake briquettes with a piece of ⅛-inch-thick sheet metal.

Another tip is to make sure the perimeter of the

Another clear canopy and forward fuselage section is vacuum-formed over the plug.

sheet is secured to a wooden frame. I staple the sheet to a piece of ½-inch-thick plywood that's the same size as the top of the vacuum box and has a large cutout in its center. If the plastic is not secured to this frame, it will be deformed (warped) when it's heated. I place the frame on top of a supporting piece of ¼-inch-thick plywood that has a single sheet of paper on top. I put this assembly on the upper warming rack of the grill and then close the lid. The supporting sheet of plywood prevents the warm, sagging plastic from touching any metal inside the grill; if it touched, it would surely melt and make one heck of a mess! The paper prevents

the hot plastic from melting onto the supporting plywood sheet.

I keep the temperature inside the grill at around 375 degrees Fahrenheit and set my timer for 3 to 5 minutes as soon as I close the grill's lid. This is not an exact science, but by using a fairly constant temperature, I can vary the "grilling time" for different types and thicknesses of plastic sheet. After 3 to 5 minutes in the grill, the plastic sheet is quite soft and ready to be quickly placed on top of the plug.

Place the plug onto the center of the vacuum box and attach the shop vac. Apply firm pressure to the frame so that it is sealed tightly against the weather-stripping, and then turn on the vac. (A foot switch or a helper comes in handy here.) After just 2 or 3 seconds, the hot plastic will be sucked down tightly around the plug; in another 20 seconds or so, the plastic sheet will have cooled enough to keep its shape.

Turn the shop vac off and remove the finished product from the plywood frame. Trim off the excess material, and that's all there is to it! You could easily make 20 or 30 duplicate canopies in an afternoon using this method.

One of these days, I'll make a larger vacuum box: maybe one that's big enough for a fuselage, but then I would have to figure out a more suitable way to heat up a really large sheet of plastic. Say ... pizza ovens are pretty big, aren't they?

Addresses are listed alphabetically in the Index of Manufacturers on page 146.
♦

Make a pop-bottle cowl
by Joe Beshar

I needed to make a thin cowl, and carving one out of balsa just wasn't practical. A modeler friend suggested that I pull one out of a clear plastic soda bottle. This sounded interesting, so I found a few clear bottles in the recycling bin and developed this simple, inexpensive procedure to make a very satisfactory cowl.

PHOTOS BY JOE BESHAR

1 Make a plug of the cowl out of balsa, hardwood, plaster of Paris, etc.

2 Use a clear plastic soda bottle into which the plug will fit as tightly as possible.

3 Cut off the bottom of the bottle and remove the cap. Insert a long dowel into the bottom of the plug.

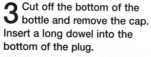
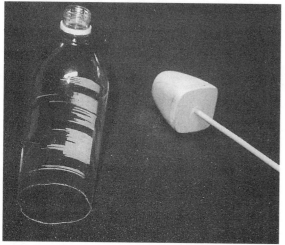

4 Put the plug inside the bottle. Direct a heat gun at the bottle while you turn the assembly.

5 The plastic has shrunk tightly against the mold plug. After it has cooled, trim the plastic and slide it off the mold.

6 Paint the inside of the cowl with plastic-friendly paint and, if you like, add a decal or two to the outside.

You can also use this procedure to make canopies and other model accessories out of plastic bottles. Good luck and happy landings!

The Bomb
by George Leu

I started this project on a whim when I missed the recycling pickup. I didn't want to take my plastic soda bottles to the recycling center, and I didn't want to keep them for another month, so I decided to do something with them. Here's how I created "The Bomb."

1 Remove the label and the colored bottom from a plastic bottle by running very hot water over them. The hot water will soften the glue and allow you to remove both.

2 Cut out two 4x4-inch pieces of cardboard; these will become the bomb fins. Slit each piece down the middle; then push one piece into the other. Insert this assembly into the 2-inch-deep perpendicular cuts that are in the rear of the bottle.

3 Use a band saw to cut the neck off the bottle and to make two 2-inch-deep perpendicular cuts in the bottle. Hold the bottle firmly as you cut; otherwise, it will vibrate too much. To prevent the fins from moving, add a seam of white glue where they touch the bottle. Let the glue dry, and spray paint the bomb flat black. Glue on a Vortac* or Hobby Lobby* bomb drop, and you're ready to dive-bomb your local flying field.

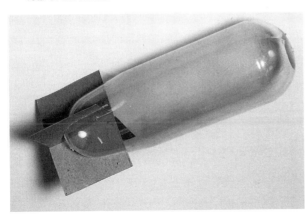

Now you're ready to create havoc at the flying field! I added some yellow pinstriping for scale effect and to help dress up the bomb. Most modelers I meet have a difficult time believing that my bomb is an inexpensive, recycled-plastic, homemade device. Try one; I'm sure you'll like it. ⊰

Pop-bottle windshield

by Randy Randolph

Plastic pop bottles have been used by modelers for windshields, cowls and fairings since they first appeared on grocers' shelves 15 or 20 years ago. The usual procedure is to make a template, trace around it on the bottle and then cut out the windshield. The photos show a way to make such a template and a more accurate way to produce a windshield from the template.

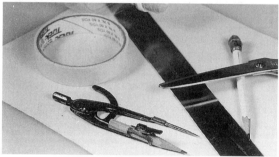

1 Other than a plastic bottle with a diameter that's close to the width of your model's fuselage, you'll need card-stock material, a compass, masking tape, a pencil, a ruler and scissors.

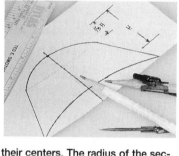

2 Measure the top of the fuselage where you'll mount the windshield. Using a compass, draw an arc of that length on the edge of the card stock. Draw another arc above the first arc, aligning their centers. The radius of the second arc should be the desired height of your windshield. Measure up ⅔ of the distance to the second arc, and draw a horizontal line. Draw two straight lines to connect the ends of the arcs. This is your windshield template.

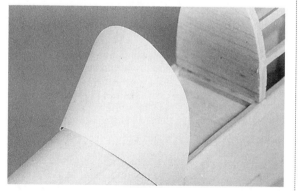

3 Cut out and fit the template to the airplane, using masking tape to hold it in place so that you can mark where it needs to be trimmed. After the template is properly positioned, mark where it contacts the fuselage.

4 Coat the back of the template with a glue stick, and glue it to the straight side of the bottle. Hold it in place with a rubber band until the glue sets.

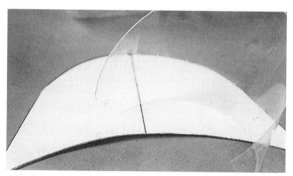

5 Use scissors to cut the windshield from the bottle, cutting exactly on the edge of the template. It's easier to cut accurately if the area containing the windshield is cut from the bottle before the windshield itself is cut. Soak the windshield in water to release the template.

6 Attach the finished windshield to the fuse with R/C56 or similar glue, and then fair it smoothly into the fuselage with the covering material used on the airplane (I used Oracover* here). To give the windshield a very realistic finish, rub a blue permanent-ink pen on the very edge of the windshield.

Addresses are listed alphabetically in the Index of Manufacturers on page 146.

Make a removable windshield

by Jim Sandquist

I needed a windshield for this Beech Staggerwing. Since I was going to paint the model and detail the cockpit, I wanted to make the windshield removable so this would be easier. The problem was how to fair it into the fuselage so that it looked scale. Here's what to do:

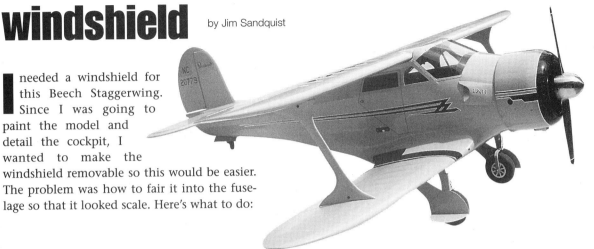

1 Make a paper pattern that fits the fuselage. Tape it in place and trim it until you're satisfied with the fit.

2 When your satisfied with the fit of the paper pattern, make one out of plastic.

3 Tape the plastic windshield into place.

4 Using your original paper pattern as a guide, cut windshield molding strips out of lightweight aluminum or printer's plate. To hold the molding in place, use small screws that will look scale on your airplane.

All that remains is to make the fairing that will hold the lower leading edge of the windshield to the fuselage. This will be accomplished using Carl Goldberg Models* Model Magic Epoxy Plus, which is flexible and can be easily formed.

5 Place masking tape on top of and ahead of the windshield to provide the shape of the fairing. Apply a film of petroleum jelly to the leading edge of the windshield on its front and back sides and screw it into place.

Apply Model Magic Epoxy Plus to the fuselage and to the plastic window. Wet your finger to smooth the fairing to shape so that it will require virtually no sanding.

When you're satisfied with the shape of the fairing, remove the masking tape. Wet your finger again and blend the epoxy into the fuselage, then let the epoxy dry overnight.

When you pop out the windshield the next day, you'll find that the epoxy will have worked itself under the plastic slightly to form an actual slot that the windshield will slide into.

6 The windshield in place. When it's time to paint, remove it. If your windshield ever cracks or gets scratched, simply cut a new windshield and replace the old one! The final product looks great, and the windshield is not only removable, but it also has a great scale appearance.

*Addresses are listed alphabetically in the Index of Manufacturers on page 146.

Install a formed windshield

by Myron Pickard

I have always had trouble shaping plastic windshields over open areas on models. Using a heat gun helps, but if you aren't careful, the plastic can easily be distorted. I decided there had to be a better way, and there is! Here's what I came up with.

Aircraft like this Ikon N'West* L-19 Bird Dog have a lot of "glass." The windshield and back window are often difficult to fit properly into place, but this technique should make it easier for you to install them.

1 Use cardboard (here, part of a cereal box) to make a template for the front windshield.

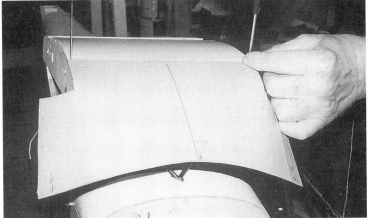

2 When you're satisfied with the template's shape, use it to trace the windshield's outline on clear plastic, and then cut the plastic to shape. Be careful to cut the inner corners smooth and round, or the plastic will crack there. With that done, screw the template into place on the model, so it will support the plastic when you use a heat gun to form the windshield.

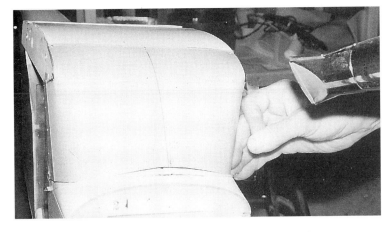

3 Remove the screws holding the top edge of the template, place the windshield material on top of the template, and then re-install the screws through the plastic and the template. (I used 0-¼ pan-head sheet-metal screws from Micro Fasteners* spaced at 1-inch intervals.) Now use the heat gun to heat the windshield along its top radius while you gently pull it into position. Do not use too much heat or the plastic will blister.

4 When the windshield has been pulled into its proper position, heat along one side while also pulling that side into position, and then secure it with a couple of screws. Repeat the process for the other side. When the plastic has cooled, finish drilling the attachment screw holes (again, 1 inch apart). Having done this, remove the windshield and the template.

5 Clean the windshield and then screw it back into position. Hold the bottom edge in place with a strip of electrical tape cut in half lengthwise. Using tape here makes it easier to remove the windshield for repairs and maintenance. For an even more authentic scale appearance, you can glue the windshield into place and add plastic-frame strips to the sides.

6 Make the L-19's rear window in the same way. It might be a good idea to save these templates in case you ever need to replace a broken or cracked windshield or window.

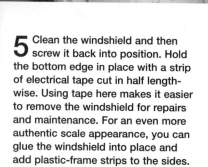

7 Here's the finished rear window. Again, I used electrical tape to hold the lower edge in place.

If, like me, you've had grief making and installing clear plastic windshields on your models, give this technique a try; I think you'll like the results.

Addresses are listed alphabetically in the Index of Manufacturers on page 146.

Frame plastic windshields

by Frederick Pope

My Royal Stearman S2N kit came complete with punch-out-and-fold acetate windshields, and I was looking for a way to make frames for them. In my vast collection of leftover good "stuff," I had half a roll of adhesive-backed, 2-inch no. 322 Nashua Duct Foil (available at Home Depot for $5.95 for a 50-yard roll). This has a finely textured finish to which paint adheres well without primer, and only gentle pressure is needed to make the adhesive stick.

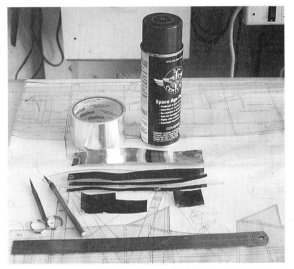

Materials and tools for simple windshield frames: a roll of Nashua no. 322 Duct Foil, fuelproof spray paint, sharp pointed scissors, no. 11 hobby knife and metal straightedge. With the paper backing still in place, painted foil is cut into strips 1mm wider than twice the desired windshield frame width.

I cut three, 8-inch pieces off the roll—one extra for experiments—and spray-painted them when I painted the engine cowl with Coverite* 21st Century High Gloss fuelproof paint to match the Coverite fuselage fabric color.

When ready to work on the 3mm-wide windshield frames, I discovered that I had to allow one extra millimeter for the thickness of the acetate and the foil fold. A no. 11 hobby knife used with a metal straightedge made crisp, straight lines through the painted foil and its paper backing. I cut four, 7mm-wide strips, peeled the paper off the adhesive backing as each strip was needed, centered the strip exactly on the acetate's edge and folded the foil over onto each side with my fingers. The result was a strongly adherent frame painted inside and out with no aluminum showing. The bottom edges of the Stearman's windshields are curved to fit the fuselage, and the folded foil followed the curves exactly.

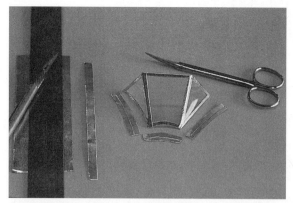

Frame footings are cut to match the curves of the bottoms of the front and side windshield frames for this experimental unpainted windshield. It's best not to make illustrative creases in the footings until the backing has been taken off and the footings have been attached to the bottom windshield frames and fuselage.

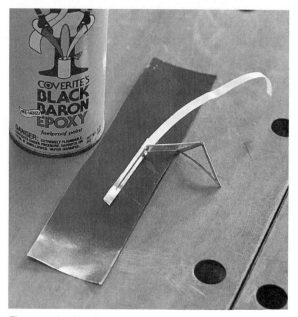

The paper backing has been partly pulled away from the frame strip on which the bottom edge of the acetate windshield is exactly centered.

Next, I tack-glued the two front and rear bottom corners of the windshield frames to the fuselage with a drop of thin CA. I made frame footings by cutting curved strips to match the bottom frame edges (with scissors) and applied these strips around the junction of the frames and the fuselage. Then I touched up any aluminum that showed at the mitered corners with a paintbrush dipped in Coverite spray paint sprayed into the can cover.

Total time spent from start to finish was about an hour.

Addresses are listed alphabetically in the Index of Manufacturers on page 146. ✦

After the backing has been completely removed, the strip is partly folded onto the acetate windshield and is then mitered with scissors to fit exactly before the fold is completed.

For the vertical front windshield frames, I used a 6mm-wide strip of foil on the outside and a 5.5mm strip on the inside, again with an exact match from inside to out. I found a single strip all the way around the top too cumbersome to fold and too difficult to miter with a pair of sharp pointed scissors, but mitering each panel piece to fit before pressing it down was easy.

4

Adding
the finer
details

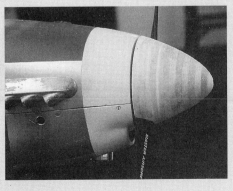

Wingtip lights for bipes

by Gerry Yarrish

The only problem with having wingtip lights on a biplane such as a Stearman PT-17 is the wiring associated with getting electricity to the top wing. Somehow, the wires have to be hidden from view. You could put the battery pack in the top wing, but then where do you put the switch so that it doesn't infringe on the model's scale outline? I like to install switches in one of the cockpit openings so that I have a clean-looking model yet still have easy access to the radio and light switches.

This technique is also a natural for other biplane designs, such as the Great Lakes trainer (FSP08742), the Bucker Jungmeister (FSP05901) and the Der Jaeger (FSP02862). Here's how I solved my wiring problem.

1 You'll need: a wiring harness from RAm Products*, a RadioShack switch (SPST), wire, a soldering iron, solder and flux, a 9V battery, 8-32 blind nuts (one for each cabane-strut mounting bolt) and steel bolts to attach the top wing. You'll also need some shrink-tubing or electrical tape.

2 During construction, drill holes in the wing ribs and install the lights and wire leads. Be sure that the wires are long enough to allow you to adjust the positions of the lights after the wing has been covered. You'll drill a hole through the wingtip and slip the lights out so that approximately 1 inch of wire is exposed on each one. Then, after covering the wing, push the wires and lights back into their respective holes and secure the lights with silicone sealant or a dab of hot glue.

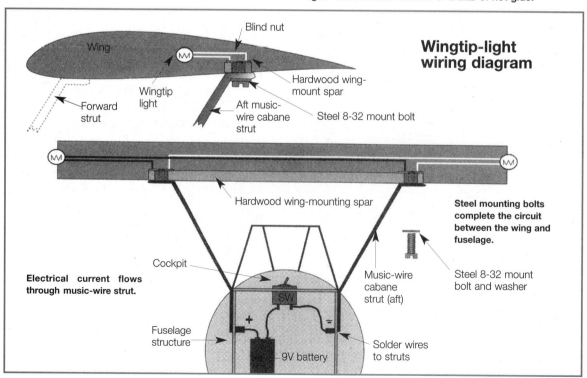

Wingtip-light wiring diagram

Wing

Blind nut

Wingtip light

Forward strut

Aft music-wire cabane strut

Hardwood wing-mount spar

Steel 8-32 mount bolt

Hardwood wing-mounting spar

Steel mounting bolts complete the circuit between the wing and fuselage.

Cockpit

Electrical current flows through music-wire strut.

Music-wire cabane strut (aft)

Steel 8-32 mount bolt and washer

SW

Fuselage structure

9V battery

Solder wires to struts

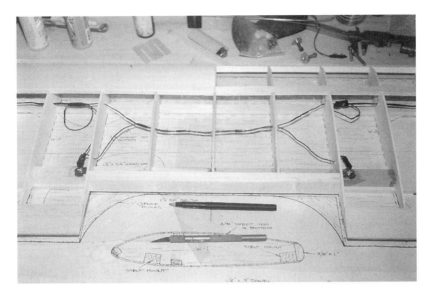

3 Back to the construction. Before you complete the wing center-section sheeting, arrange the wires neatly as shown, with the positive leads of each wingtip light at the left, aft, cabane-attachment blind nut and the negative leads at the right, aft blind nut. Notice that I used short pieces of shrink-tubing to bundle the wire leads neatly into place. Any excess slack in the wiring can be looped as shown. Don't tension the wires too much, or vibration could cause the solder joints to fail.

4 Clean the surface of the blind nut and apply some soldering flux. Heat the blind nut with a soldering gun, and solder the wire leads into place. Now, with both positive and negative leads soldered, complete the wing's center-section sheeting and cover it.

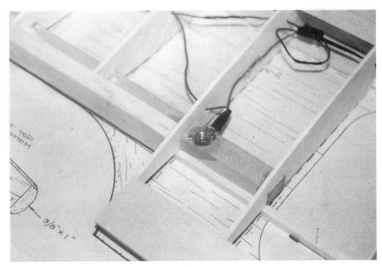

5 When the wing is bolted into place on top of the music-wire cabane struts with steel bolts, the wing-wiring circuit is extended into the fuselage. Electrical wires are also soldered to the bottom of the aft, music-wire cabane struts. These wires are attached to the 9V battery and the lighting system's on/off switch. The illustrations show this system in detail and should make it easier to understand.

When the wing has been painted and balsa fairings have been added to the cabane struts, the model looks neat; no unsightly wires are visible between the top wing and the fuselage. There are no wire connections to attach, and there's no chance of a connection failing (unless the wing comes off in flight, in which case you won't be worrying about the lights anyway!). This wiring setup has a simple design, is easy to make and requires virtually no maintenance. Try it on your next biplane or parasol model, and watch your friends go nuts looking for the wires. Enjoy!

Addresses are listed alphabetically in the Index of Manufacturers on page 146.

Add running lights to your model

by Glenn Bolick

With all the emphasis on building more and more scale-like models, one of the least expensive and easiest to implement—but least often done—scale features is running lights. With today's LEDs, it's not difficult. All the components can be purchased for less than $10 at any RadioShack or electronics store. Further, installation is simple and quick.

Photo 1 shows the necessary components: wire, resistors, LEDs and a switch (not shown are grommets, blind nuts, wing-attachment screws and solder). Photo 2 is a view of a framed-up ½A Hobby Lobby Super Cub with a blinking red beacon LED on top of the fuselage and another on top of the rudder. Photo 3 shows the green LED mounted to the right wingtip, while photo 4 shows the resistors and grommets wired to make the wing's electrical connection.

To get power to the wing, the battery is connected to the wing hold-down blind nuts via the switch in the fuselage. Metal grommets are embedded in the wing and used to continue the connection to the wing. Solder the left and right LED leads to two grommets through which metal screws are used to mount the wing. In this way, current may flow through the blind nuts and into the wing circuit to light the wing LEDs. The LEDs mounted on the fuselage are connected in parallel. For a plane this size, 4-40 bolts and blind nuts are appropriate, as are the smallest grommets I could find at the hardware store. Use larger hardware for larger planes.

See the schematic for wiring details, and note that each LED has its own resistor wired in series to limit current flow to specified levels. My Cub is electric-powered, and the motor power battery is wired to the switch and provides the necessary power to energize the LEDs. For glow-powered planes, a 9V cell or other battery source must be installed. When 9 to 12 volts are applied, 560-ohm resistors must be used in each LED line. If, on the other hand, 4 to 6 volts are used, 330-ohm resistors are more appropriate.

Note that a yellow light is specified for the rudder, as RadioShack does not stock the white LEDs that are preferred; the effect, however, is the same. I think you'll find that the comments you get on the field will more than justify the little time required to do this installation.

MATERIALS

RadioShack part numbers

LEDs	Small	Large
Red	276-310	276-214
Green	276-303	276-215
Yellow	276-021	276-205
Blinking red	276-036	RSU10524437

Resistors
560 ohm: 271-1116 (for over 6 volts)
330 ohm: 271-1113 (for 6 volts or less)
Switch: SPST sub-miniature 275-406
Wire: 24-gauge stranded 278-1301
Grommets, blind nuts and screws are available from hobby shops and hardware stores. Use sizes to suit your aircraft.

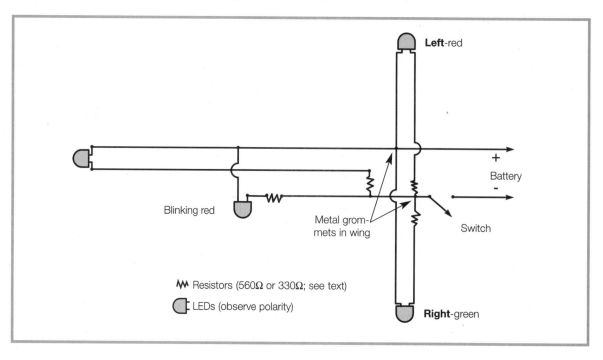

Left-red

Battery
+
−

Blinking red

Metal grommets in wing

Switch

Right-green

⋀⋀ Resistors (560Ω or 330Ω; see text)
◖ LEDs (observe polarity)

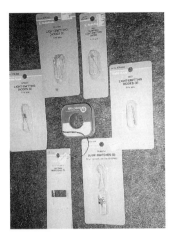

Photo 1, left: the major components are available from RadioShack.
Photo 2, above: here, the blinking beacon and rudder LED are visible.

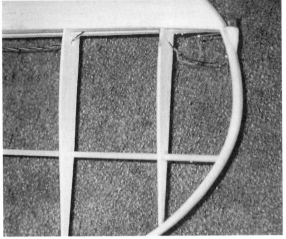

Photo 3: the installation of the wingtip LEDs is straightfor-
ward; the balsa housing should be made to suit the particular
aircraft being modeled.

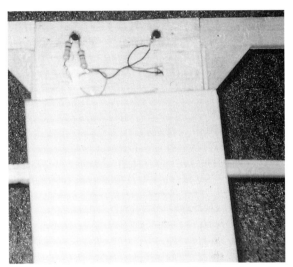

Photo 4: the metal grommets are glued into the wings after
the wires and resistors have been soldered to them.

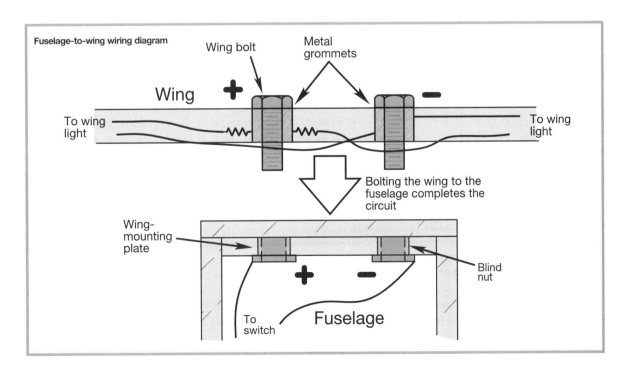

Fuselage-to-wing wiring diagram

Apply rivet detail

by George Leu

Applying scale rivets to your model airplane requires understanding and experimentation to achieve satisfying results. The technique you use to reproduce them will vary depending on your skill level and the level of detailing you're comfortable with.

When stand-off-scale judging was restricted to a 15-foot distance, scale modelers finished their aircraft to show details that could easily be seen from that distance, e.g., larger-than-scale rivets and panel lines. Rivets reproduced on a ⅙-scale model would probably have been the size of half a grapefruit on the full-size aircraft. The intention was to make it easy for judges to see rivet detail.

Today, almost all scale model competitions allow static judging to be done within 1 to 4 feet for the purpose of observing craftsmanship and details. There's no longer a need for modelers to exaggerate rivet size. Of course, this also means that judges can now see whether the proper type of rivet has been reproduced, be it a flush, braiser-head or pop-rivet. Let's take a closer look at rivets and application techniques.

RAISED RIVETS

To obtain the appearance of standard, run-of-the-mill raised or braiser-head rivets, I like to use a mixture of white glue and water. Any white glue will yield satisfactory results, but I prefer to use Formula 560 from Pacer Technology*. When mixed approximately half and half with water, this glue produces rivets that won't shrink or show concavity when they've dried. I can't say this for other glues I've used.

Depending on how much water you mix with the glue, you can produce larger or smaller rivets. A thick mixture will produce a large, tall, rather obvious rivet head, and a thinner mixture will produce a much less obvious, smaller rivet head. Rivet size is generally dictated by the scale of your model, and it's up to the modeler's discretion.

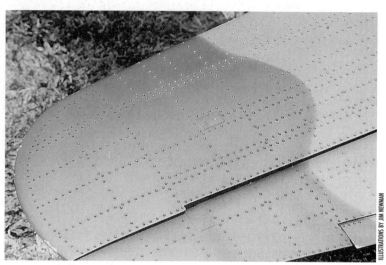

Rivets—especially ones with raised heads—are part of almost every scale model you might want to build. Once you learn the technique, adding them to your model is easy.

ILLUSTRATIONS BY JIM NEWMAN

PREPARATION

For best results, apply your rivets after the primer has been sanded smooth and all your panel lines have been applied, but before you paint. Practice makes perfect, so get a piece of butyrate sheet material, and try the following methods on it before you try them on your model.

METHODS

There are many ways to apply rivets, so experiment, and develop your own technique. They can be applied using a hypodermic syringe, a toothpick, a common pocket comb, or a Riveter Stencil from Innovative Model Products (IMP)*. For each of these methods, you must first draw a reference line with a soft pencil to guide your row of rivets.

• **Hypodermic syringe.** First, cut off the sharp, angled tip of the needle to form a blunt 90-degree end. Use some fine sandpaper to remove any burrs from the tip. Next, fill the syringe with your mixture of glue and water. The trick is to exert just enough pressure (with your thumb on the plunger) to produce only one drop at a time; too much pressure will produce a stream. You want to produce one drop of glue every second or so.

Do not touch the tip of the hypo to the model's surface; just allow the glue drop to come in contact with it, and let the model's surface pull the drop away from the end of the needle. Space the rivets about ³⁄₁₆ inch apart, and try to develop a comfortable rhythm. Don't rush; just concentrate on

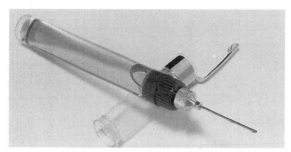

Another very good applicator for glue-drop rivets is a fine-tipped pocket oiler such as this one (available from the R/C car department at your local hobby shop). Just clean out all the oil before you fill it with your water/glue mixture.

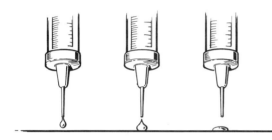

Using a hypodermic syringe is the classic way to apply glue-drop rivets. Notice that the needle does not touch the model's surface while the glue is being applied.

spacing the drops evenly along the reference line. Move your entire hand in a motion that's parallel to the reference line. The nice thing about using glue for rivet heads is that, if you mess up a rivet head or the spacing, you can simply wipe it away with a damp cloth and do it over.

When you've finished, stand back and see how you've done. If you like the result, let it dry, and then apply a light coat of paint. After you've practiced a bit, go on to your model, and work on a section at a time until you've finished. I bet you will

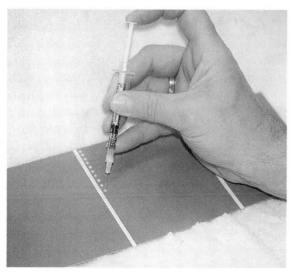

Before you apply rivets to your model, practice on a scrap piece of plastic.

be pleasantly surprised at the success you'll have right from the start.

If you can't find a suitable hypodermic syringe, another option is to get a squeeze bottle similar to the one shown in the drawing of the IMP Riveter Stencil. Fine-tipped oiling tubes are also acceptable for riveting. Just make sure you clean all the oil out of the tube before you fill it with glue.

• Toothpicks and combs. Some modelers prefer to apply rivets by dipping the end of a toothpick in glue, applying the rivet, then wiping off the end of the toothpick and repeating the process. As with the hypo method, don't allow the tip of the pick to touch the surface of the model. This method allows you to spread out and shape the rivet a little after it has formed; this works especially well for giant-scale models, but it's more time-consuming than the syringe method.

To speed up the process, some people use pocket combs to apply many rivets at once. A fine-toothed pocket comb is, essentially, a long row of evenly spaced toothpicks. Breaking the comb into small sections and applying six or more rivets at once works better than trying to use the comb at its full length. Dip the comb's teeth into glue, and then gently apply them as mentioned above. Like the toothpicks, the comb should be wiped clean of glue before the next row of rivets can be applied. I find it helpful to break off every other tooth to prevent the glue drops from touching each other.

• **Riveter Stencil.** This is a relatively new product for applying rivets, and it might be the easiest way to go. It has a lot of potential for scale modelers. The stencil strip is about 13 inches long and 1 inch wide. It comes with one or two rows of evenly spaced holes punched along its length. The stencil is first placed on the surface and aligned with the reference line. Because the stencil is made of thin, clear plastic, this is very easy to do. Tape the stencil into place, and then apply a thin bead of glue along the row of punched holes. Then, with a small squeegee or a piece of scrap balsa, smear the glue over the row of small holes to fill them, then carefully lift the stencil. What's left is a row of evenly spaced, uniformly sized glue dots. When you apply rows of rivets close to one another, it is best to let the previous row dry before you continue so that the stencil doesn't smear the rivets you've already applied.

I have just started to use this product, but the results look very promising. I find that the size and spacing of the rivets are more suitable for ⅙- or ½-scale models, but I have seen the stencil used effectively on a ⅕-scale Spitfire.

A little trick you can use after your rivets have dried is to lightly run 360-grit sandpaper over their heads to take off a bit of the hard edge. Sometimes, I'll mix a little color into the glue mixture so that the rivets will have a worn look when I sand over them during the weathering process. Again, practice and experimentation are the keys to developing a method that best suits your tastes.

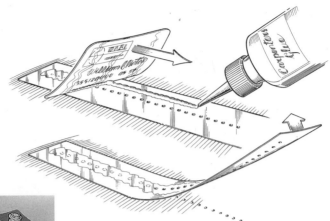

The Riveter Stencil is very easy to use. Tape it into place, apply glue over the hole, smear the glue evenly along the strip's length, and then lift the strip for a row of perfectly spaced rivet heads.

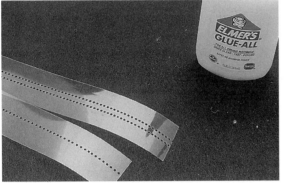

The Riveter Stencil by Innovative Model Products is a new way to apply rows of uniformly placed rivets to your model.

All these methods will yield excellent results, but remember that each takes time and practice. When you've become comfortable with one of them, or when you've developed your own method, your model will be elevated to a new level of scale accuracy. Instead of being just a nice, scale model, it will be a true miniature aircraft. Details make the difference.

You should note that more than one kind of rivet is used in aircraft construction. For example, on the leading edge of, say, a Spitfire, raised rivets would not be scale, because flush rivets would be used in this area of the wing. Always look carefully at your documentation first.

Addresses are listed alphabetically in the Index of Manufacturers on page 146. ✦

Make scale, multi-panel windshields

by Gerry Yarrish

Scale open-cockpit models have one thing in common: windshields. Whether they use simple wrap-around or multi-panel windshields, models need this detail to look complete. Here is a simple way to reproduce a good-looking, scale, multi-panel windshield for your next open-cockpit airplane.

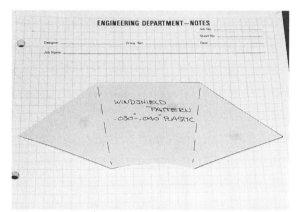

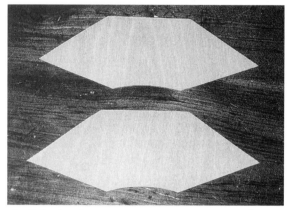

1 Most plans will have a flat template for the windshield appropriate for your model. If you are scratch-building, use some card stock or stiff paper and develop your own pattern. Here is the pattern included with my Ziroli/Aeroplane Works* PT-17.

2 Following the template, draw the pattern onto 1/32-inch-thick plywood. Because the Stearman PT-17 has twin cockpits, I've cut out two windshield blanks. These will be used to produce the framework for both windshields.

3 Draw the frame outlines and the corner seam lines on the blanks. Using a sharp modeling knife, cut partway through the blanks along the seam line. Do not cut all the way through; you simply want the cut to act as a hinge so that you can cleanly bend the blank along the corner seams as shown.

4 Wrap a piece of paper over the cockpit opening and tape it into place where the windshield will be seated. Place the windshield blank over the paper and trace its bottom outline where it comes into contact with the paper. This outline will serve as the centerline for the bottom edge piece of the finished windshield.

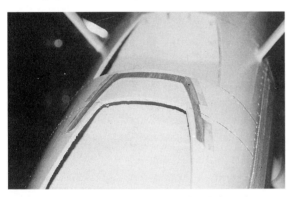

5 Remove the paper from the model and draw the outer edges of the bottom edge piece around the centerline about ⅛ inch all around. What you will end up with is a U-shaped pattern, as shown. Trace the pattern onto ¹⁄₃₂-inch-thick plywood and cut out the bottom edge piece. Tape the U-shaped edge piece into place on top of the fuselage. Note that the fuselage is finished and painted before the windshield is built.

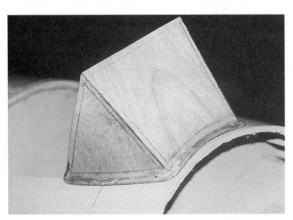

6 Place the bent windshield on top of the bottom edge piece, and glue it with CA. The bottom edge of the windshield should be placed on the centerline. Note that the windshield assembly is now quite stiff and holds its shape.

7 Drill ³⁄₁₆-inch-diameter holes in each of the windshield-panel corners.

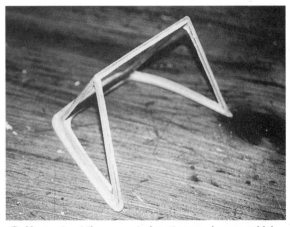

8 Now cut out the unwanted center panel areas, which will leave the thin framework shown here. I used a thin cut-off wheel in my Dremel* Moto-Tool to do this quickly and precisely. Now glue three, ³⁄₃₂-inch-wide edge pieces to the aft edges of the windshield. These edge pieces strengthen and stiffen the finished windshield.

9 Along the bottom edge of the windshield, make a fillet of hobby filler that blends the bottom edge with the vertical windshield frames. Let the filler dry and sand it smooth with 320-grit sandpaper. Sand the entire windshield again and prime it with two

coats of wood primer. I used F&M Enterprises* Feather Coat. When everything is dry, sand again and re-prime if necessary until you have a smooth, grain-free finish.

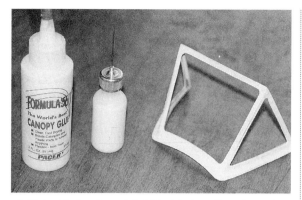

10 I added surface detail (rivets) along the edges of the bottom edge piece and the center of the frames. I used Pacer Technology* Formula 560 mixed 60:40 with water and applied the mixture with the IMP* squeeze bottle shown. Let the "rivets" dry overnight.

11 Paint the finished windshield frame with a color that matches your model. I used F&M's Poly Tone paint applied with a Badger* Model 150 airbrush. Paint the entire frame (inside and outside edges), and let it dry.

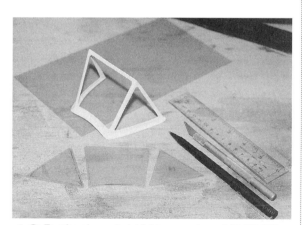

12 For the clear windshield panes, I used Sig* 0.030-thick, clear-plastic sheet. Place the framework over the plastic, and trace its inside edges onto the plastic. Do not remove the plastic's protective covering, but trace onto it. Cut out each of the panes, leaving approximately ³⁄₃₂ inch all around the traced lines.

13 Next, remove the protective material only on the side that comes in contact with the framework, and glue the clear plastic into place one pane at a time with Pacer Technology Formula 560. If you leave the inside of the plastic pane protected with the protective covering, you'll be able to use lead weights to hold the pane in place while the glue dries without fear of scratching the clear plastic. Repeat the process for each of the remaining panes.

14 When all the windshield panes have been glued into place, remove the inside protective material, and glue the completed windshield framework into place with Formula 560. That's it! Stand back and admire your handiwork. When added to your model along with a scale instrument panel, a scale pilot bust and some padding around the cockpit opening, windshields add much to the realism of any scale model. Give it a try; you'll be pleased with the results.

*Addresses are listed alphabetically in the Index of Manufacturers on page 146.

Make nacelle fairings
by Joe Beshar

From as far back as I can remember, blending and filleting surface intersections have always been a problem for me. Having searched many avenues for a simple and practical method, I succeeded in developing a satisfactory way to apply fairings and fillets and would like to pass it on in hopes that others will find the method as helpful as I have

1 At the fillet or fairing location, position a block of Styrofoam about 1/8 inch below what will be the final contour. (You can use several pieces of Styrofoam as further trimming after assembly; it's a simple matter.) Glue the foam in place with aliphatic white glue, and trim as necessary.

3 After the Model Magic has set, use 60-grit sandpaper to trim the filler and 120-grit for final contour and finish. After final sanding, wipe or blow off the residual dust.

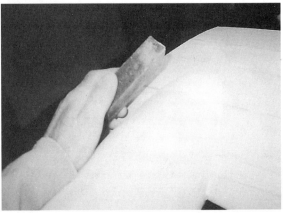

2 With a spatula, spread Model Magic* liberally into the recessed area. Model Magic is easy to apply, lightweight and easy to carve and sand.

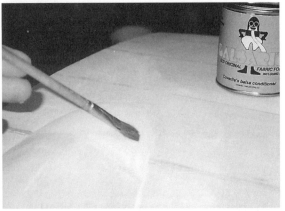

4 Coat the fillet or fairing with Balsarite*. This will glaze the surface to make it compatible with practically any final finish, from heat adhesive coverings to paint.

*Addresses are listed alphabetically in the Index of Manufacturers on page 146.

Make a dummy radial engine

by Bud Gewinner

The Stearman PT-17 is a classic biplane that should be modeled often, but you've got that big problem of a radial engine staring you right in the face. When I decided to build a 50-inch-span Stearman, I knew I couldn't hang a single, naked cylinder on its front end. Of course, I could have put a cowl on the model and called it a "Super," but then it wouldn't have been a Stearman PT-17. I could have bought a radial engine, but even forgetting about the cost, that isn't really the answer for a moderate-size model. I knew I had to produce four dummy cylinders that realistically matched my O.S.* .52 Surpass 4-stroke. I've flown this model for a full summer, and engine vibration hasn't damaged the dummy assembly.

INTERIOR CYLINDERS

All dimensions given here are for the .52 Surpass, but you can easily determine the correct dimensions if you're using a different engine. Start by making the dummy cylinder's interior tubes. Cut four pieces of 94x40mm, 1/64-inch-thick ply with the grain parallel to the short side so the plywood will bend more easily. Soak the pieces in boiling water for 15 to 20 minutes, then bend them around a 1 1/8-inch-diameter wooden dowel. Wrap them tightly with an elastic bandage. The next day, glue

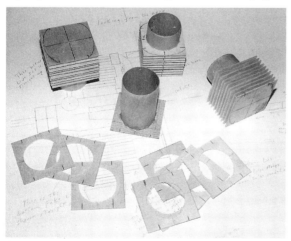

The dummy cylinders at various stages of construction.

their edges together to form four tubes. This isn't easy, but if you wrap some wax paper around a 1-inch-diameter dowel and put it in a vise, you can hold the bent ply while you tack it in a few places with medium CA. Then, hold the cylinder down on a sheet of wax paper and run a full bead of CA down its length. Don't worry if the tube isn't perfectly round; it will be forced into round when you slip the fins on later.

"COOLING" FINS

Now make the fins: use 36, 42x40mm pieces of 1/32-inch-thick ply. Draw a 1-inch circle in the centers of four of the fins and cement a tube in the center of each. Use a 1-inch circle cutter on a drill press to cut a circle in each of the remaining 32 fins. (If you don't have a drill press or a 1-inch circle cutter, sand the centers out using a Dremel*.) Then, sand the holes until the fins just slip onto the tubes, which are about 1 3/16 inch in diameter. You're now ready to cement the fins onto the tubes. Just set the tube down on its top fin, slip a fin down on the tube and tack it with medium CA. Use scrap 3/32-inch brass as spacers so the fins are evenly spaced. Each dummy cylinder should have nine fins on it. Don't worry if the holes in the fins aren't perfectly round and there are gaps between the fins and the tube; you won't notice these in the completed engine.

The dummy cylinders now have to be sanded so that the fins have rounded corners. Just look at the fins of your engine and try to duplicate their shape.

Here are one of the blocked-up cylinders and the brass strip that I used as a guide. An A-frame support is also shown. You can also see how the inner end of the 1/64-inch-diameter tube is cut away to clear all parts of the engine and engine mounts.

One of the fully finished cylinders and the valve cover, the aluminum tubes, the rocker box and the balsa support for the inner end of the aluminum tubes.

DUMMY CYLINDERS

Now you're ready to assemble the cylinders. First, build the firewall that you will actually use in your plane. I used 5mm-thick, 5x5-inch-square lauan plywood that I later trimmed to a 5-inch-diameter circle. Drill 1/8-inch holes in the center of the firewall and in a large board, then slip in an 1/8-inch-diameter dowel to keep them together. Then, draw lines radiating from the center of the engine; these represent the centerline of each cylinder. For a 5-cylinder radial, those lines would be 72 degrees apart. Mount your engine to the firewall and place it back on the board (you'll have to drill holes in the big board to allow the bolts of the engine mounts to pass through). Don't use an oversize mount because it might interfere with the wood cylinders. I used Sig* aluminum mounts (drilled to reduce weight) because they're nice and compact.

Each dummy cylinder will be glued to an A-frame that's bolted to the firewall. To determine the proper height of the A-frames, take one of the dummy cylinders, place it in position and block it up until its height matches your engine's "live" cylinder. I made a simple metal guide that I placed over the crankshaft, and with the plug out of the engine, I rotated it from the engine to the dummy cylinder. Now make four A-frames, as shown in the drawing. Make sure that the dummy cylinder clears all parts of the engine and engine mounts by about 1/8 inch, so the engine doesn't touch anything when

it runs. Don't worry how this inner area looks; after the crankcase cover is put on, you won't see it.

Fasten the A-frame supports to the firewall. Place the A-frames on the firewall so that they straddle the 72-degree lines, and set them so they are about 3/8 inch away from the outer diameter of the firewall. Later, you'll have room to glue a balsa lip onto the firewall; this will make the engine look "built in." When the A-frames are in place, transfer the hole positions to the firewall and drill and tap for 4-40 nylon bolts. Now bolt all four A-frames to the firewall and fit each dummy cylinder by sanding away as much of the 1/64-inch plywood end as necessary; the outer fin of each cylinder should extend to the same point as the outer fin of the engine. The metal pointer can be rotated to each cylinder to determine if each is positioned correctly.

You're now ready to cement each cylinder to its support. This requires some care to get each cylinder lined up properly on its radius line. Use 5-minute epoxy on the top of the A-frame, then set the cylinder on the support and quickly make sure it's lined up in the proper direction and that the top fin is the proper distance out. When the 5-minute epoxy has set, go to the next cylinder, but don't try to do them all at once; you don't want to "nudge" the previous cylinder when you start to work on the next one.

VALVE TRAIN

Now you are ready to set up the valve train. You'll have to make the valve cover, the aluminum tubes, the rocker box and the balsa support for the inner end of the aluminum tubes. Measure the rocker box that sits on the top fin. (The .52 Surpass measures 32x24mm.) To make these units, use two pieces of 1/32-inch ply with three pieces of 3/32-inch balsa that are slightly smaller. Sandwich the pieces together and glue them. You'll have to drill 3/16-inch-deep holes in the bottom of these rocker boxes to accept the two pushrod tubes, which you'll make out of 3/16-inch aluminum tubes. Glue these rocker boxes to the top of each cylinder and be certain that the holes are in the proper position for the aluminum tubes. The support for the pushrod tubes at the inner end of each cylinder is simply a piece of 1/8-inch balsa glued to the bottom fin. Cut two notches into the balsa to accept the two aluminum tubes. To make the four 1/8-inch balsa supports, cut eight pieces of 3/16-inch aluminum tube of the length needed to go from the rocker box to a little beyond the bottom fin where the balsa support will be. The height of the balsa pieces should be determined by test-fitting the aluminum tubes so their height is the same as those of the real cylinder. When the fit is OK, glue the balsa supports to the dummy cylinder, but do not glue the aluminum tubes in yet or you will have trouble painting the cylinders later. The valve cover is sim-

The almost fully assembled engine (before painting) and the cover piece that represents the front of the crankcase of a radial engine.

ply a balsa piece sanded to the right shape. Don't glue the tubes and valve cover in place until the cylinders have been painted aluminum.

FINISHING UP

The cover piece will represent the front of the radial engine's crankcase. It slips over the real engine's crankcase boss, just behind the propeller drive washer and is attached with a homemade clamp made of 0.020-inch aluminum. I made my

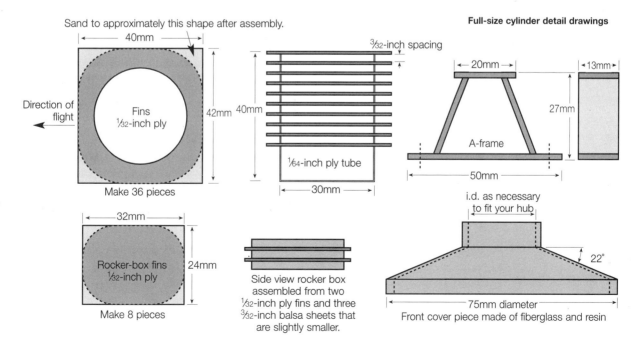

Sand to approximately this shape after assembly.

40mm

Direction of flight ←

Fins 1/32-inch ply

42mm   40mm

Make 36 pieces

32mm

Rocker-box fins 1/32-inch ply   24mm

Make 8 pieces

3/32-inch spacing

1/64-inch ply tube

30mm

Side view rocker box assembled from two 1/32-inch ply fins and three 3/32-inch balsa sheets that are slightly smaller.

Full-size cylinder detail drawings

20mm   13mm

27mm

A-frame

50mm

i.d. as necessary to fit your hub

22°

75mm diameter

Front cover piece made of fiberglass and resin

Right: the result. If you think the "live" cylinder is the one facing you with the factory "O.S." valve cover, you're wrong! The live cylinder is to the right. I bought an extra valve cover so the top two cylinders (the only ones you really see in detail) would look authentic.

cover piece of fiberglass, but you could also solder a 0.005- or 0.010-inch brass cone onto a tube that has a diameter that enables it to just slip over the crankcase boss.

Now you're down to cosmetics. Unbolt the dummy cylinders and remove the aluminum tubes that were installed temporarily. Paint the cylinders aluminum and the A-frame supports black. Paint the balsa valve cover aluminum or black to match the color of the valve cover of your "live" cylinder. Paint the crankcase cover plate black.

If your "live" engine has become discolored from use, you'll want to "antique" the dummy cylinders. Use thinned black or dark brown paint and a small brush to touch up the fins until they match.

The final step is to reassemble the engine. Now you can glue in the aluminum pushrod tubes. Just push one end into the hole in the valve box and, using CA, glue the other end into the supports that you attached to the bottom fin of each cylinder. When you do this, be sure that the tubes of each cylinder are parallel and that the height of the tubes at this support is the same as that of the "live" cylinder.

You can add a little more realism by cutting some 2mm-thick disks from a ³⁄₁₆-inch wooden dowel. Paint them black and use CA to glue them onto the cylinder heads to represent the head bolts. Paint some of these aluminum, too, to look like the crankcase bolts.

You are now ready to remove everything and build the firewall into the fuselage. When you build the fuselage, it's best to extend a lip of balsa about ½ inch beyond the firewall. This will make the engine look "built-in" and will hide the cylinder supports.

You've now saved yourself the cost of a multi-cylinder, radial engine, added only 2.75 ounces to your Stearman PT-17, and your model looks like the real thing. Good flying!

Addresses are listed alphabetically in the Index of Manufacturers on page 146. ▲

Build a mock rotary engine

by Martin Irvine

PHOTOS BY MARTIN IRVINE

I needed to build a ⅛-scale dummy 80hp LeRhone for a 1915 Nieuport 12, but nothing commercially available would do the job. Every idea I came up with to build the finned cylinders seemed to be a tremendous amount of repetitive work or was likely to achieve a second-rate result—until this one. This basic method can be used for other scales and engines. The big plus is that although the fins are very thin, the structure is pretty sturdy.

The dummy crankcase is a piece of a mailing or drafting tube. If you can't find a suitable tube, make one by rolling brown packing paper, and use glue sparingly.

The "cylinders" are red cardboard tubes cut to length (as long as the cylinder is high—from crankcase to cylinder head). Cap the cylinder ends of the tubes with ³⁄₁₆-inch sheet balsa and sand them to match the crankcase curve using sandpaper wrapped around the large tube.

Cut the fins out of a manila file folder. Cut the outer circle first. On the LeRhone, the outer diameter of the fins changes, so about a third of the circles should be slightly larger than the rest. Now cut out the inner circle. This has to be slip-fit over the cylinder, so take your time to get it right. If it's too

tight, the fin will become distorted when you put the cylinder on; if it's too loose, it will be difficult to glue into place.

Place the fins on the cylinder one or two at a time (align them using the plastic cap), and glue them into place with a drop or two of CA. Continue this process until you reach the top of the cylinder.

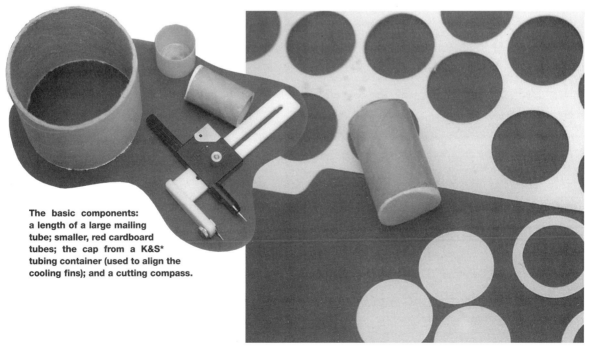

The basic components: a length of a large mailing tube; smaller, red cardboard tubes; the cap from a K&S* tubing container (used to align the cooling fins); and a cutting compass.

The fins are cut out of a manila file folder.

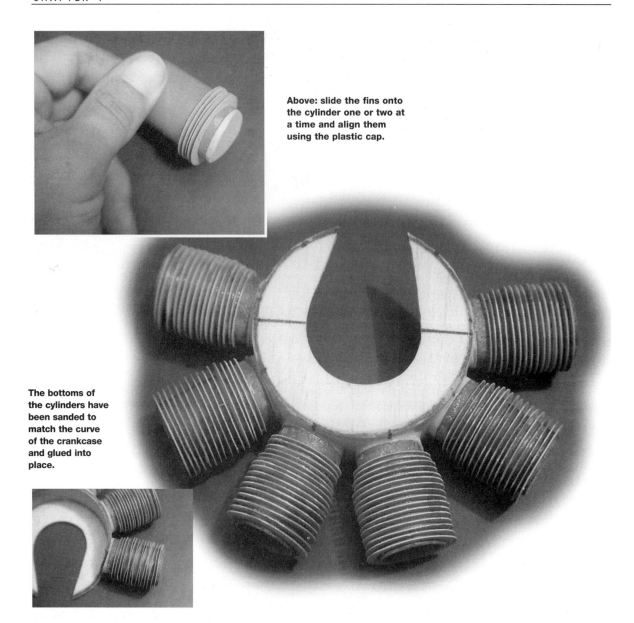

Above: slide the fins onto the cylinder one or two at a time and align them using the plastic cap.

The bottoms of the cylinders have been sanded to match the curve of the crankcase and glued into place.

Make the rest of the cylinders in the same way.

The front of the crankcase is balsa. I added another piece of ¼-inch balsa to the front and sanded it to a conic section to simulate the front of the LeRhone. I spaced the cylinders 40 degrees apart because the real LeRhone has nine cylinders (only six show). Be careful when you place the cylinders; the human eye can pick up even small discrepancies.

I mounted the finished project in the Nieuport cowl. The cylinder heads can be made out of ⅓₂- or ⅟₆₄-inch plywood disks with ⅓₂-inch plywood fins. The valves and pushrods are dowels, and the other bits are basswood. The intakes are modified parts left over from another kit, but you could easily carve or mold them.

I painted the dummy engine with a mixture of silver and black and painted the intakes copper. The next step is very important: go over everything with a wash of brown/gray thinner. I used the muck left over from cleaning my brushes.

When you're faced with a task like this, regard it as a model in itself. Breaking it down into its component parts turns it into a less daunting task. An evening in front of the TV will get the cylinders finished; it will take another evening to finish the structure, followed by an hour's painting; then it will be ready for mounting.

Addresses are listed alphabetically in the Index of Manufacturers on page 146.

Securely mount a Williams Bros. dummy radial
by Richard La Porte

When I decided to bash a Sig* Hog Bipe into a Stearman, I had one difficulty to overcome. How could I duplicate the exposed radial engine that's so characteristic of this beautiful aircraft? In 10 years of modeling, I had never read anything on how this could be done effectively.

After analyzing the problem, I concluded that it had to be attacked in two steps: I had to build the dummy radial and fit it to the actual engine, then make a cowl between the firewall and the rear of the dummy radial.

ENGINE CONSTRUCTION

I used the Williams Bros.* Wasp scale kit for the dummy engine. It has nine cylinders instead of the seven usually found on Stearmans, but the diameter was about right for my model.

I didn't build the rear of the engine and left off everything aft of the intake manifold. After experimenting with various glues, I found that medium CA with a bit of kicker worked better than anything else on the plastic.

When the front of the dummy radial was complete, I mounted it on an O.S.* .70 4-stroke and trimmed it until it fit properly at the prop shaft. I had to cut two cylinder heads away about 50 percent to provide an ⅛-inch clearance between the dummy and the actual engine.

I carefully measured and recorded the distance

Williams Bros. scale Wasp engine kit. The rear of the engine housing is left unfinished.

between the firewall and the dummy radial's intake manifolds. This determines the length of the cowl.

COWL CONSTRUCTION

I removed the O.S. .70 and the dummy, then I installed a jig on the engine mount to represent the real engine and provide a centerline for the cowl. I slid a round template of the same diameter as the dummy onto the dowel of the jig, making sure it was the correct distance from the firewall.

Using the template as a guide, I made the cowl out of a ½-inch-diameter balsa ring surrounded by 1/64-inch-thick aircraft plywood. I epoxied light fiberglass onto the outside of the plywood for strength and installed short sections of ⅛-inch dowel through the balsa ring. These dowels were later mated to holes in each intake manifold and hold the dummy radial on the cowl.

I then fit the cowl to the O.S. .70 engine and muffler and drilled a hole for the high-speed needle valve. When the fitting had been completed, I painted the cowl silver at the front and covered it with MonoKote* at the rear. I also drilled four mounting holes.

I attached the dummy radial to the cowl with PFM* because it helps to damp vibration. A separate piece of the cowl is permanently attached to the area just aft of the O.S. .70 cylinder head. It remains in place whenever the cowl and dummy radial are removed.

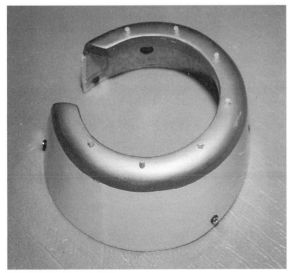

The fiberglassed cowl is ready to accept the dummy engine.

The dummy engine is attached to the cowl via holes drilled in each plastic intake manifold.

The right side of the cowl showing the permanently installed section behind the O.S. engine.

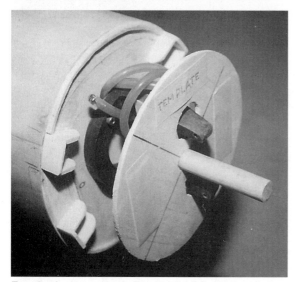

Top: the dummy engine is fitted to the O.S. .70 4-stroke.
Center: this jig is used to maintain the centerline.
Above: this round template is used to guide cowl construction.

AT THE FIELD

During 25 flights, I have only been bothered by one problem: the two dummy cylinders that I had cut away to fit around the O.S. .70 kept falling off. I eventually ran dowels to each cylinder from the cowl ring. I installed the dowels at an angle and anchored them to the rear of the half cylinders with PFM. After I had completed this modification, the assembly held together very well—even during a few nose-overs on landing! The dummy radial looks great and really makes this model stand out.

Addresses are listed alphabetically in the Index of Manufacturers on page 146. ✦

Resin radials
by Carl S. Diehl

My newest scale model is a Pica/Robbe* Waco bipe. I wanted to do a good job because I planned to take it to the annual Gator Shootout. A scale, dummy radial engine was a must, so I decided to resin-cast one.

Saito* 4-stroke engines have very realistic one-piece cylinders and head castings that make good "generic" cylinders for round engines. It's relatively simple to resin-cast copies of the Saito "jug" and then use them to make 3-, 5-, 7- and 9-cylinder dummy engines. Here's how I did it.

1 Before a casting can be made, the cylinder openings need to be plugged. I used wooden dowels to seal the pushrod holes and the cylinder base holes. I used a plastic cap plug (from the junk box) to seal the exhaust opening.

2 Next, I made a female mold of the cylinder with Bondex plaster of Paris (available from art-supply stores). I cleaned the plaster away from the rocker-arm cover bolts prior to removal. Notice that a little less than half of the cylinder is embedded in the plaster.

3 Clean out holes in the back of the plaster mold so you can insert ⅛-inch-diameter "knock-out bolts." These holes should be located over the original Saito ejector-pin holes for their cylinder casting.

4 Insert some old bolts in the holes, and tap them lightly with a small hammer to force the Saito cylinder out of the mold.

5 The plaster mold reproduces the surface detail of the Saito cylinder exactly. For a more accurate full-size engine look, I cleaned up the fin depressions in the mold.

6 Here are two polyester-resin castings that were made using the plaster mold: the one in the background is as it came out of the mold; the one in the foreground has been cleaned up, and the base (which is no longer needed) has been removed.

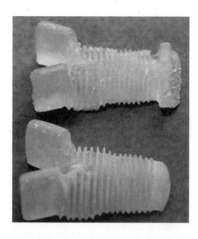

7 Next, use the cleaned-up resin cylinder (with ejector-pin tubes installed) to produce a second-generation mold. Before you make the new female mold, the cylinder must be waxed and coated with mold release (PVA). Notice that the master cylinder is glued to a flat, smooth back piece. The ejector-pin tubes serve the same function as the holes in the original plaster mold.

8 The second mold (shown here with master cylinder removed) is also made of polyester-resin. A dam is built around the master, and the resin for the mold is poured over it and allowed to cure. To prevent cracking, mix the resin so that it cures slowly.

9 Resin that will form the cylinder for my dummy engine has been poured into the new mold. Wax and PVA are also required inside the mold so that the new castings can be removed. After repeating this process seven times, I have enough cylinders for my dummy radial engine.

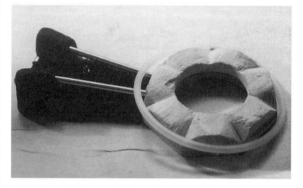

10 I made the crankcase hub out of ½-inch balsa and added a ¼-inch-ply backplate for strength. Here, the first finished and detailed cylinder (notice pushrod tubes and spark-plug detail) has been set into position and glued to the hub. The ignition-wire ring is made of plastic tubing.

11 For proper cooling during flight, I made the two dummy cylinders that were in line with my Laser 200 engine's cylinders removable. This rear view of the radial engine shows the brass tubes and screws that are attached to the removable cylinders. One button-head screw holds each cylinder in place.

12 The completed dummy radial is in place on my ⅕-scale Pica/Robbe Waco bipe. As you can see, the removable cylinders are still in place and cover the Laser engine nicely.

14 The two removable cylinders have been removed for flight. The cylinders for the Laser 200 can just be seen. Cooling has been very efficient with this setup.

Addresses are listed alphabetically in the Index of Manufacturers on page.146.

13 With the radial installed in the cowl, the model looks great, and the Laser engine is completely out of sight. The dummy engine is simply glued to the inside of the cowl with Zap-a-Dap-a-Goo*.

Easy pilot headphones

by Carl S. Diehl

While completing my latest project, a Midwest AT-6/SNU, I needed a set of headphones for the rear admiral pilot. Having none on hand for a ⅕-scale pilot, I did what any scale builder does: improvise!

PHOTOS BY CARL DIEHL

1 Two pills in their plastic containers, a rubber jartop remover from the kitchen and rubberized drawer-liner material are all you'll need.

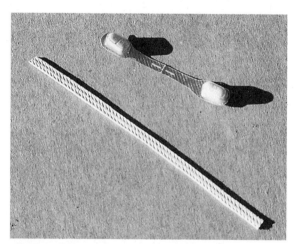

2 The pill packs have been cut down to retain the backing and set the shape of the headphones. Use a strip of the drawer liner for the head strap.

3 Cut the pill packs apart at the separation line, and CA them to the strip of liner. The assembly will stretch to fit over the pilot's head.

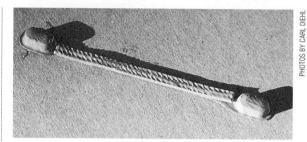

4 Paint the headphones only with water-based (acrylic) paint (or the pill packs might be distorted or dissolved).

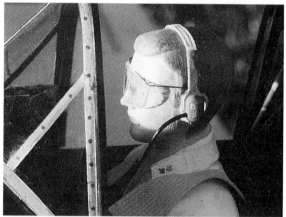

5 The finished product is CA'd to the ears of my ⅕-scale Williams Bros.* pilot. If you like, you can also use CA to attach a piece of rubber-covered wire to one of the earphones and to the dashboard. Note: my 1940 SNJ-2 was piloted by Rear Adm. Aubrey Fitch, who was the commander of the Carrier Division I during 1941 and flew from the USS *Saratoga*; therefore, I used a sportsman-type pilot with a white shirt, etc.

Addresses are listed alphabetically in the Index of Manufacturers on page 146.

Reproducing pop rivets and screw heads
by Bob Underwood

How about that airplane! It's exactly the model you've been looking for! True, it's a home-built, but the lines are pleasing, and the color scheme is striking. You've already got a good 3-view for it, and the owner would love to have you model his creation. The airport is right in your hometown! What more could you ask for? Where's the camera?

A set of circumstances like this seldom happens. Usually, the aircraft is inaccessible, the only one ever built crashed 60 years ago, the owner isn't willing to cooperate, etc. So there must be a catch to your find. Often, the "catch" is some element that is difficult to duplicate in model form.

WHAT'S THE CATCH?

So what was the catch to this find? Being a home-built, it is liberally sprinkled with pop rivets and Phillips-head screws. Now, there's a chance that if you build the model to just the right scale, you might be able to locate Phillips-head screws that match the ones used on the full-size plane. The operative word is "might"! And that should be preceded by the words, "If you're really luck,y you …"

These Phillips-head screws around the windshield of my Hiperbipe are actually fake! Painted silver to resemble a metal finish, they add lots of realism to the completed model.

The tools used to punch out pop rivets and screw heads. A metal block with a slot cut into its side and a hole drilled through it works great as a punch die. I use 0.010-inch-thick plastic from Sig to make the rivets and screws. Also shown is a modified Phillips-head screwdriver used to emboss the heads of the replicated screws.

When it comes to finding a 1/4-scale pop rivet to duplicate the original, the phrase "lots of luck" becomes wildly optimistic.

So-o-o, you're going to dump the project? No way! Just make your own Phillips-head screws or pop rivets in any size head you need! Notice I said "head!" That's because you aren't really going to produce an actual screw or rivet, but will fake the head so your model will look like it's held together with those types of fasteners. Remember, creating a scale model more often than not is an illusion. It's not always reality.

FAKE SCREWS AND RIVETS

It was a neighbor (a non-modeler, I might add) who helped me develop the technique for producing screw and rivet reproductions. I had tried a variety of techniques involving glue drops and stamping processes to simulate the heads. For one reason or another, none of these proved satisfactory. The neighbor, Dick, suggested the heads be punched from some material. Actually, he even provided the metal block with a slot for a die.

The next step was to determine the diameter needed for the screw or rivet-head representation. If you were thinking ahead when you first saw the subject aircraft, then you probably measured them.

Along the leading edge of the Hiperbipe's aileron (also at its tip), pop rivets complete the scale illusion. Again, they're made of punch-out, thin plastic disks.

If not, some form of guesstimation may have to suffice. At this point, you may be subjected to your first lesson in "scale psychology." As far as surface detail is concerned, it is almost always better to understate rather than overstate the representation. In short, keep it smaller. This becomes even more true as the model becomes larger. The viewer becomes more sensitive to detail items in a ⅓-scale model than on a ¼ or ⅕ scale. You can argue "exact" all day, but people (even modelers) have a real hangup when you try to explain that a model is "⅓ the size of the original." They often have problems comprehending the concept. When their eyes see screws and rivet heads that are the correct size, their brains see them as too big.

Now, let's drill a hole in our metal piece that we will be using for a die. Run the hole right down through the slot and out the bottom of the block. At this point, you need a metal piece to act as a punch. A simple solution will be to use the drill bit you just ruined by running it too fast, with no lubricant, through the hard metal block! (Ah, yes, experience can be such a valuable teacher!)

Next step? Let's find something to use to punch out the representations of the heads. My search took me through a variety of "stuff," including litho plates, foils, etc. What worked? I found that the 0.010-inch plastic material sold by Sig Mfg.* was perfect. I slid a piece in the slot, placed the chuck end of my ruined drill bit in the hole, tapped it with a hammer, and a little, round, dome-shaped piece popped out the bottom of the metal block. Actually, I found it necessary to dress the end of the drill a bit to achieve the right amount of "dome-ness" on the plastic piece. You can form a pan or rounded head, or whatever is required.

Onward! Now that I had a bunch of little, round, domed pieces of plastic, a means of attachment had to be devised. (Actually, at this stage, they really didn't look like pop rivets!) The process that ultimately developed was to drill a hole, using a tiny numbered drill in my Dremel*, wherever a rivet was to be placed. You'll have to experiment a bit, because the diameter-to-rivet representation and the straight pin used to apply it are factors in how big the hole needs to be.

I used the straight pin to flip the piece over (remember, they come out of the die, domed side down) and then picked it up by pricking it with the pin point right in the center of the dome. A very small amount of glue (such as Pacer's* Formula 560) was applied to the back of the piece. Centering the plastic piece over the hole, pressure was applied to the pin, and that pushed the point into the hole. With the correct amount of pressure, the plastic will collapse in the center, leaving a ring that looks like a pop rivet. It sorta looks like one half of a somewhat flattened bagel.

MINI PHILLIPS

To create a Phillips screw head, it is necessary to find a cheap (the cheaper the better) Phillips screwdriver with a shank that is larger in diameter than the hole in the metal block. Grind or file the tip of the shank so that it just fits the hole, but bottoms out with the tip below the slot in the block. Grind

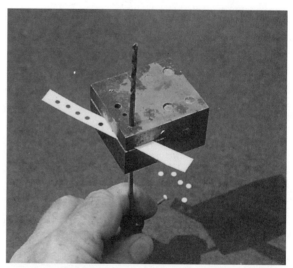

To make Phillips-head screws, place the modified screwdriver in the bottom hole and the drill-bit punch in the top hole. The screwdriver is ground down so it bottoms out below the slot in the die block, and it requires two taps with a hammer to make a duplicate screw head.

or file off the point of the tip, and carefully dress the + portion to the proper size of the Phillips + mark. It takes some experimentation.

To make a Phillips-head representation, follow the same process as for the pop rivet, but place the ground-down shank in the hole from the bottom of the block, support the metal block and screwdriver in contact with your workbench, and tap twice with the hammer. The first tap will punch out the head, and the second one will imprint the + representing the Phillips slots. Glue it on the same way, except you won't need to predrill a hole. Neat, huh?

RIVETING THOUGHTS

1. The Sig plastic is white, so if your aircraft is white, you're home free. If it isn't white, then experiment with when to apply the rivet/screw representations during the painting process. Quite frankly, if you are one who lavishes copious paint on a model, you may have a problem.

2. If the rivet/screw heads are left in a natural metal state on the full-size aircraft, then paint the plastic with silver or aluminium paint before you punch them out.

3. You may want to experiment with other glues; however, the RC 560 allows the most latitude in adjustment and replacement. I tried CA and found it problematic.

4. Punch out the heads in small quantities (maybe 10 to 20 at a time), then apply them. It breaks up

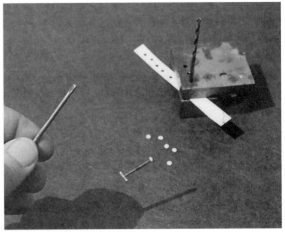

To properly emboss the plastic screw heads, the tip of the Phillips-head screwdriver must be ground or dressed with a file to remove the point of the cross.

the tedious nature of each part of the job. For the rivet heads, you can punch out a half dozen or so before you push them through the metal block. The Phillips are, of course, a one-at-a-time operation.

5. If you have allergies, find somewhere to direct your sneeze other than at the pile of punched-out heads! Weighing practically nothing, they will scatter to every recess of your workshop with even a modest ka-choo! I've been there—done that!

6. How about time? Yep, they take time to produce. I suspect the total time from beginning to end figures out to about one minute per head. My most recent Hiperbipe project consumed about 10 hours. Not worth it, you say? Have you ever thought about Pattern?

And to end with a thought for the day: plan ahead; remember, you can't cut the piece longer!

Addresses are listed alphabetically in the Index of Manufacturers on page 146. ✦

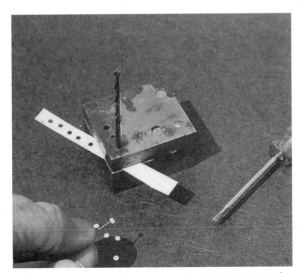

A future scale pop rivet ready to be glued into place on the model. The pop rivet look is accomplished by pushing the pin point through the plastic disk and into a previously drilled hole in the model where the final rivet will be located. It takes practice to learn how far to push the pin for the desired effect.

Custom-build a scale spinner

by Vance Mosher

I t can be hard to find a spinner that's the right size and shape for your scale model even if you're building a P-51. It's even more difficult to find a spinner that's more than 3 inches in diameter, much less the correct shape. Manufacturers of most P-51 kits reduce the model's nose diameter so that they can find a commercial spinner to fit the kit. If you have a model other than a P-51, you usually don't even get that far.

It's easy to make a scale spinner. I've used the following technique to make spinners for a Top Flite P-51, an 86-inch-span Zero and a 36-inch-span Westland Wyvern. I made the Zero spinner of basswood and the others of balsa. The largest was used on a SuperTigre 3000 and the smallest on an O.S. .10. That range ought to cover everything. White pine and basswood are more durable (fortunately), and balsa is lighter. Use balsa to make spinners for up to about .60-size engines; use harder woods for larger engines.

IN THE WORKSHOP

You do need to know the correct size and shape of the spinner in your scale. The place to find that is the scale 3-view, but also measure the front end of your model. To scale a small drawing to the correct size, set a copy machine to the largest magnification and re-copy your 3-view's spinner a few times until you get close. Then do some arithmetic to figure the

The finished spinner on a Top Flite P-51.

last scale-up and copy it to the correct size. The lines will be blurry and too thick, but you can redraw it reasonably by hand.

Make a few copies of your drawing. Glue one onto card stock for a template and draw lamination lines on the other, per the diagram. Cut out the inside of the template. The lamination lines are ¼ inch apart for ¼-inch-thick wood and are used to determine the correct diameter for each wood lamination. This saves you a lot of sanding and a lot of wood, too.

I made the spinner shown in the photos on a drill press because a lot of people don't have access to a lathe. Use the fastest turning speed possible for a rounder, smoother spinner.

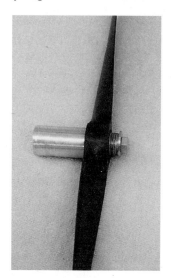
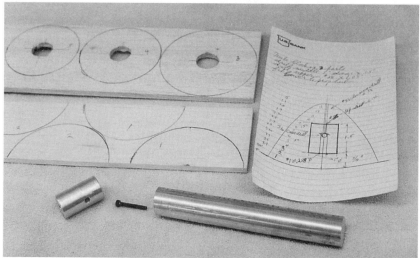

Left: the bar-stock prop nut is bolted to the propeller. Right: bar-stock prop nut, lamination guide and balsa with large spinner pieces.

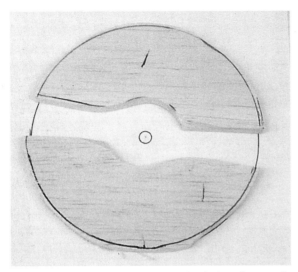

The first laminations are centered on the circle and are ready for the propeller.

You'll also need a 6-32 tap, a tap handle, a no. 36 tap drill, two bolts, a nut, a few washers, a tap of the same thread as the one on your engine crankshaft and a suitable tap drill (e.g., the Saito .91 on the P-51 uses a 7x1mm tap and a $^{15}\!/_{64}$ tap drill). The tap-drill size is listed on the tap package. Get the longest bolts you can find in the correct size.

Find a piece of hard aluminum bar stock that's approximately 1½ inches long. (It can be as small as 1-inch long with a ⅜-inch diameter for a .10-size engine.) You can also use a smaller spinner screw in smaller engines. Drill and tap the prop thread about 1 inch in on one end and the 6-32 thread about ½ inch in on the other end. Be sure the ends of the bar stock are square to the sides and flat before you drill them; a disk sander works well for this. Accurately locate and center punch the ends before drilling. (All of this is easier on a lathe, of course.) Square and hexagonal bar stock will work, too. Cross-drill this new prop nut to clear a piece of ⅛-inch music wire, which you can use as a bar to tighten the nut on the prop. A good place for the hole is about 1 inch out on the nut, at the end of the prop threads.

Consult your drawing and cut all of the wood laminations to the correct diameter with a bar-stock-size

hole in the middle of the big ones. Use only partial pieces up to the thickness of the prop hub. Fit the hub pieces closely to the prop hub, with the grain of the first lamination parallel to the prop. The prop should fit firmly into the spinner. The top hub lamination should be just thick enough to clear the top edge of the prop hub. Set the spinner properly on the prop from front to back; you can shim it later. The bottom of the spinner will line up with the back edge of the prop, flat on the table. This makes the spinner fit closely to the front of the cowl without having to leave room for a spinner backplate. Don't try to fit the laminations under the prop; if you do, you won't be able to get the spinner off the prop later.

PUTTING IT TOGETHER

Bolt the bar-stock prop nut to the front of the prop. Shim everything up with scrap wood after this because the bolt head sticks out of the back of the prop. Glue the lamination on the face of the prop to the stack with the grain running perpendicular to the prop. Slide this lamination,

Add hub laminations until they clear the top of the propeller.

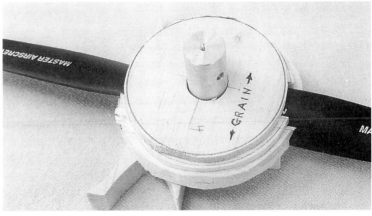

The hub laminations and the first prop-nut lamination are shimmed with scrap wood.

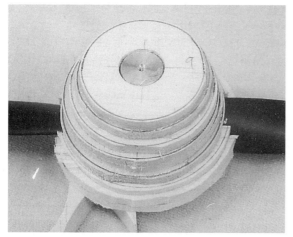

The laminations up to the top of the prop nut.

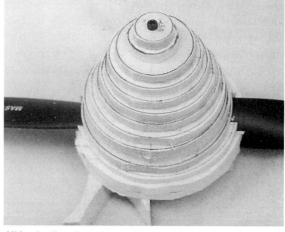

All laminations have been added, and the 6-32 bolt has been installed.

and the next several, over the prop nut to ensure that they will line up inside the finished spinner. Continue the laminations, gluing each one with the grain at a right angle to the previous one, until you clear the top of the prop nut. Don't get glue on the prop nut!

Center-drill a $\frac{5}{32}$-inch-diameter hole into the laminations above the prop nut to clear the 6-32 spinner bolt. The very front lamination is center-drilled $\frac{7}{32}$ inch to recess the head of the spinner bolt. Slide each of these laminations onto the bolt before gluing, and screw the bolt a little way into the spinner nut to line up the laminations while the glue sets. Glue each lamination with the grain at a right angle to the previous one. Don't get glue on the bolt, either.

Remove the 6-32 bolt. Pull the prop nut and the

prop out of the laminated spinner. If you weren't careful with the glue, you can either twist the prop nut out with a wrench on the prop-shaft bolt, or under extreme circumstances, heat the prop-nut bolt with a propane torch or a large soldering iron until the glue debonds. Don't breathe the heated glue fumes!

Saw the head off the duplicate prop-shaft bolt and screw and lock it into the spinner nut with the extra prop-shaft nut. Tightly reassemble the spinner, the 6-32 spinner bolt and the prop nut. Leave the prop off and make sure that the spinner doesn't slip on the spinner nut. After the spinner had cured, I added a layer of thin epoxy to the inside of the spinner-bolt cavity to make it fit tightly into the spinner.

MAKING SAWDUST

Chuck the prop-shaft bolt into your drill press and sand the spinner until you get a smooth curve that just touches the edge of all the laminations. If you have cut the laminations accurately, they will provide a template for the correct shape of the spinner. The safest thing, though, is to sand close to all of the laminations, then turn the drill press off and use the template for final shaping. Do all the sanding with a large, heavy sanding block (a piece of 2x4 works well) to minimize "bounce" and get a truly round shape. The cross-grain laminations help, too. Use 50-grit sandpaper for initial sanding and 120-grit to finish.

Cover the front face of your prop with plastic food wrap. Pack the ends of the blade cutout in the spinner (not in the

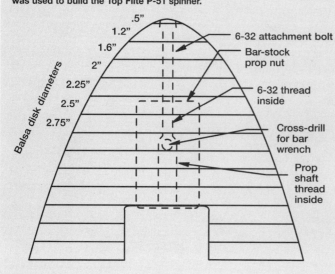

Figure 1. A sample template and laminations guide. This one was used to build the Top Flite P-51 spinner.

center) with Model Magic* or lightweight spackle and bolt the prop into the spinner. The spackle should completely fill in around the front of the prop at the edges of the spinner. Fill any voids in the surface of the spinner, too, and set it aside to dry. The prop will come out of the spinner when the spackle is dry, thanks to the plastic wrap.

Replace the shaft bolt in the spinner and gently sand the spackle smooth on the drill press. Make sure that the spinner is just a bit smaller than the front of the airplane when it's mounted.

FINISHING TOUCHES

Coat the spinner (including the back) with finishing resin or thinned epoxy and then add a few coats of fiberglass and a lot of thick, excess resin. This is easier if you cut the fiberglass into "spinner-size" triangles. Put the shaft bolt into the plastic-wrapped prop hub, place this assembly partway into the spinner and clamp it into a vise to hold the spinner upright while the epoxy cures. This helps to balance the spinner. Punch the bolt through a sheet of paper and cover the vise with the paper to prevent excess epoxy from dripping onto the vise.

After the epoxy has cured, trim the glass and put the spinner back into the drill press and sand it smooth at high speed with about 220-grit paper. Paint it and you've finished. This spinner is easy to paint, the paint won't chip off and there's no bare metal back edge. Balance the spinner; weights glued into holes in the rear face work well, but don't get too close to the edge. One way to balance a big spinner is to hang it on a string from its center, like a plumb bob. It will hang level if it is balanced. The spinner will probably be close to balanced to begin with.

This spinner only needs some paint.

The spinner on the Top Flite P-51 only weighs 3½ ounces—about half the weight of a commercial unit—and it's a lot tougher. It's the right shape, too. It also cost a lot less, and it was fun to build—a great combination with immensely satisfying results. Plus, I was able to build something that no one else has.

Addresses are listed alphabetically in the Index of Manufacturers on page 146. ✦

Make scale antennas

by Jim Sandquist

Small details are often the difference between an average-looking model airplane and a really special one. Many subjects have antennas that are difficult to reproduce, and some sport models can be greatly enhanced by scale-looking antennas.

I used the process shown here on my ¼-scale Stinson L-5, which took first place at the Toledo Aviation Show in 1995. It isn't very difficult.

1 Cut out the needed components. The oval base and side support are cut out of ¹⁄₁₆-inch-thick plywood. The ¼-inch-diameter dowel is approximately 1 inch long. Determine the antenna length and, depending on the scale size needed, cut it out of 2-56 or 4-40 wire.

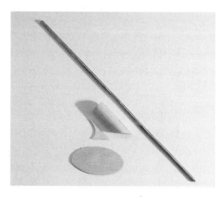

2 Use a drill press to drill a hole through the center of the dowel so that the antenna wire has a snug fit.

3 Glue the plywood base components together with CA.

4 Use Carl Goldberg Models* Epoxy Plus to blend everything together. This two-part epoxy can be shaped and smoothed out easily with wetted fingertips. Very little sanding is required once it has set. Mix the two parts of the Epoxy Plus in equal amounts, and spoon the mixture into the areas that you want to blend together. You will have approximately 10 minutes of working time before it has set. Smooth out the epoxy with a wet finger. After it has dried thoroughly, finish-sand it, prime and paint.

PHOTOS BY JIM SANDQUIST

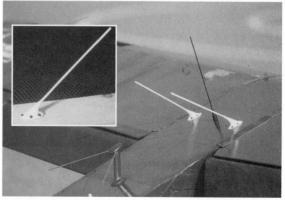

5 Drill holes in the base for the mounting screws, and screw the mount into place on your model. The threaded part of the screws below the base can be cut off, and if you like, the base can simply be glued into place. The final product looks very convincing, and it replicates the antennas used by the full-size general aircraft industry on a variety of planes. Good luck!

Addresses are listed alphabetically in the Index of Manufacturers on page 146.

Make vintage wheels out of jar lids
by Roy L. Clough Jr.

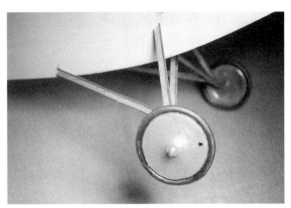

The next time you spread the last of the marmalade on your toast, chuck the jar and save the lid; it can be the foundation of a vintage aircraft wheel. These easy-to-make, lightweight wheels add an authentic touch to scale-type models of the 1930s and earlier.

Start by finding the center of the cap and punching an ⅛-inch-diameter hole. The best way to locate the exact center is by lightly grasping the lid in a three-jaw lathe chuck. If you have a good eye, the center dimple is a good guesstimate. There's also the trick of scribing several lines with a small square moved around the diameter; the lines will intersect in the center.

Sand a small spot around the axle-bearing hole so the solder will stick to the lid, but leave the rest of the paint or lacquer coating in place; it makes a great primer for the rest of the job. Solder a bearing of K&S* tube into the hole. The photos show an ⅛-inch bearing, which will turn nicely on a 3⁄32 wire axle. Slip a balsa spacer block over the axle bearing, push the fender washer into place and solder them together. Now spin the wheel on a short axle wire, and correct any wobble by gently bending the assembly until the wheel tracks true. Next, puddle thin or medium CA between the ends of the spacer block and the metal parts and set it aside overnight.

I use Skyloft*, a tough, non-woven nylon, for the wheel fabric. Cut a piece that will project about 1 inch around the rim, then make a small hole in its center for the wheel bearing. Soak the Skyloft in water and pat it until it's merely damp. Coat a washer with tacky craft glue, and stick the damp material into place. Run a bead of tacky craft glue around the outer periphery of the wheel, and work the fabric into it, stretching it slightly to form a wrinkle-free cone. Smooth the glued-down circumference, but don't worry about the overlap bumps you'll get here and there. Let this dry overnight.

In the morning, the wheel should have a nice, drum-tight cover. Check the edges to be sure that they are stuck down, and work a little tacky glue into any spots that look thin. Coat the fabric two or three times with clear butyrate dope. When it has dried, apply your favorite color to both the fabric side and the original, lacquered metal back. If you want to gild the lily, simulate valve access by punching out a small disk of black paper then sticking it

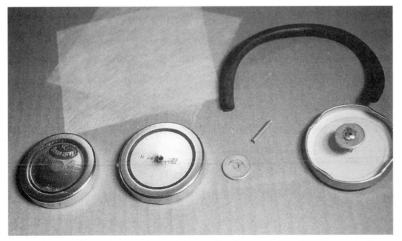

Everything you'll need to make a vintage wheel: a metal jar lid (shown in three stages of assembly), a washer, a short brass tube, Skyloft material and neoprene tubing.

After you've punched a hole in the lid, a metal tube, a balsa block and a fairing are soldered and CA'd into place.

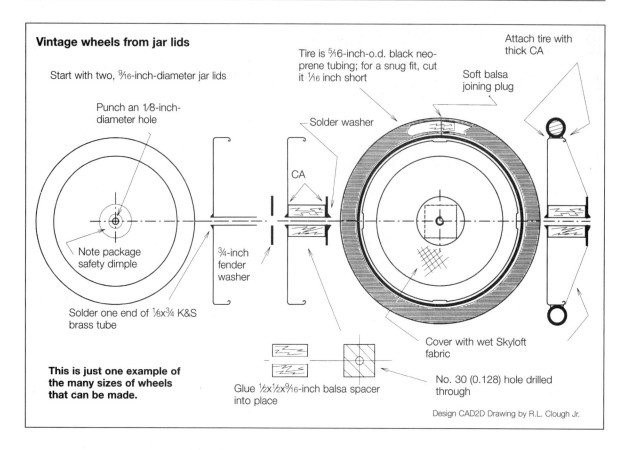

Vintage wheels from jar lids

Start with two, 9/16-inch-diameter jar lids

Punch an 1/8-inch-diameter hole

Note package safety dimple

3/4-inch fender washer

Solder one end of 1/8x3/4 K&S brass tube

This is just one example of the many sizes of wheels that can be made.

Tire is 5/16-inch-o.d. black neoprene tubing; for a snug fit, cut it 1/16 inch short

Solder washer

CA

Attach tire with thick CA

Soft balsa joining plug

Cover with wet Skyloft fabric

No. 30 (0.128) hole drilled through

Glue 1/2x1/2x9/16-inch balsa spacer into place

Design CAD2D Drawing by R.L. Clough Jr.

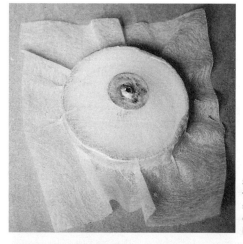

Skyloft fabric is stretched over the lid.

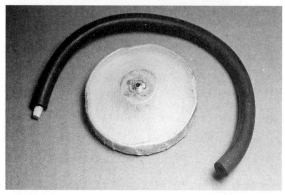

Neoprene tubing with a soft balsa joiner makes a great tire to glue around the wheel.

to the doped fabric near the rim.

The tires are made of black neoprene tubing (available in many sizes in most hardware stores). Wrap the tubing around the wheel and mark the needed length. Trim the ends of the tubing at a slight angle, but cut the tubing about 1/16 inch shorter than the circumference of the wheel. Make a joiner plug of soft balsa and use it to center the ends of the tubing when they are CA'd together. (Some might use a kicker with the glue; I don't because I've never had one of these tires come apart.)

Give the CA plenty of time to set up. Then roll the joint with thumb pressure to mash the balsa plug inside, and the joint will become practically invisible. Now slip the tire over the wheel. It should be a fairly snug fit, but it need not be tight.

Spin the wheel, adjusting it until the tire is centered as well as possible, then run a bead of thick CA cement around both sides where the tire meets the rim. Set the wheel aside in a horizontal position until the CA has set.

As noted on the plan sheet, different diameters of jar lids, fender washers and K&S tubing allow a fairly wide choice of wheel sizes. Finished wheels are suitable for lightweight models up to 30 to 35 ounces.

*Addresses are listed alphabetically in the Index of Manufacturers on page 146.

Make lightweight spoked wheels

by Gordon Bradt

PHOTOS BY GORDON BRADT

Spoked wheels are not just for the old and slow flyers anymore! They can be as big as you want and yet still be quite rugged. Best of all, they are easy to build. What's the secret?—monofilament spokes, wire-coil rims and the use of my vanishing wheel jig.

MATERIALS

Here's what you need:

• Six feet of ⅛-inch, soft-aluminum grounding wire (available at places like RadioShack), or two, 36-inch sticks of ⅛-inch, soft-aluminum welding rod (for small wheels, use ³⁄₃₂-inch aluminum rod).

• About 4 inches of ⅛-inch-i.d. x ⁵⁄₃₂-inch-o.d. brass tube (or larger, if your axles are larger than ⅛ inch in diameter).

• Four no. 8 brass washers.

• 25 feet of 25- to 50-pound-test monofilament fishing line.

• For the jig fixture, one 36-inch stick of ¹⁄₁₆-inch brass brazing rod.

• Tire material (that, we will talk about later).

• Thin CA, epoxy and silver spray paint.

1 Form the rims. For a mandrel, find a piece of PVC pipe that is about ³⁄₁₆ inch smaller in diameter than the rims that you want to make. Clamp it in a vise,

and then use some vise grips to clamp one end of the aluminum grounding wire about ¼ inch in from the pipe's end. By hand, tightly wind the aluminum wire around the mandrel, making sure each coil is snug against the one before.

Wind eight coils; you'll use only six, but you will lose part of one coil as the wire springs back, you will scrap uneven ends, and you may need a spare in case of a goof. Now cut six good coils; if necessary, taper their ends with a file to accept a ³⁄₁₆-inch length of the ⅛-inch-i.d. brass tube as a splice.

2 Make the hub tubes. Cut two 1¼-inch lengths of the ⅛-inch-i.d. brass tube for the hubs, then cross-drill four, ⁵⁄₆₄-inch holes in each tube. Stagger these holes about every 20 degrees. The hole locations are not all that critical; just keep them toward the center of the tube and far enough away from each other to avoid having two holes become one oval hole.

3 Make the jig fixture. Solder the brass washers about ⅜ inch in from the ends of the hub tube. To hold the hub tube, make the small fixture base shown in the photo. On the base, mark lines for half as many spokes as you will have on one side of the wheel. I like to build 48-spoke wheels, so I mark the fixture with 12 line positions like a clock face. For purists, I think the French used 40-spoke wheels and the British used 64 spokes.

Now lay each rim down on your fixture base, and use a felt-tip pen to make a mark at each of the 12 hour positions. For ready visibility when winding, extend the marks around and over to the other side of the coils.

• The vanishing jig. Cut eight lengths of the ¹⁄₁₆-inch brass welding wire for the jig. The pieces of wire should be about ¼ inch longer than the diameter of the rims that you have made. Round the wires' ends to make handling them more comfortable. Insert three of these wires through the hub tube, position the rim hoop, and slightly bow the wires to hold the rim in position. The idea is to secure the rim concentrically inside the hub tube and perpendicular to it. Do this by turning the assembly and jockeying the rim and wires until you have minimized the run-out, or wobble. If you need to, add the fourth wire for more support. Also keep the jig wires away from the pen marks where you will wind the spokes. You can slightly bend the jig wires to get the rim to stay where you want it, but don't sweat it. This is not brain surgery. If you end up with 1/16-inch run-out, only your onboard pilot will notice. I don't have my jig wires all alternately overlapped or evenly spaced. Temporarily apply pressure to hold the rim in place, then apply CA to the joints where the jig wires cross the rim. When you have the rim where you want it, apply CA to the hub tube. Don't have anything stuck inside the end of the tube when you apply CA to that area, or it will be permanently stuck to the tube. If you want to support the tube, stick it in a hole, not over a pin.

• Winding the spokes. This is the fun part. The winding takes only about a minute, so if you drop a stitch, or miss a mark, or the "spokes" aren't taut enough, just unwind and start over.

Start by tying the monofilament line with a single twisted loop at one of the marks on the rim (say, the 12-o'clock position), and put CA on the knot. Let the CA dry, then

hold the assembly and start to wind the line down around the hub and back up to the 1 o'clock mark, over the top and back down around the hub on the other side and on up to the next mark (2 o'clock), and so on. Be sure to wind around the hub in a U-shape; don't cross the line over itself. Keep it taut while you wind by using one of your fingers to clamp it to the rim. When you get back around to 12 o'clock, cinch the line around a few times and CA it into place. Check and adjust the line to be sure it crosses the rim at each hour mark, and then CA all the contact points.

Now look to see whether any of the fixture wires are in the way of the half-hour positions (halfway between the contact points). If any are, gently break the wires free at the rim, slightly bend them out of the way, and clean off the dried CA. Now simply repeat the winding sequence, but go halfway between the hour marks. I don't bother to mark these half-hour points; just eyeball them. CA all the half-hour-mark contact points and where the line loops around the hub tube on each side.

4 The jig vanishes. Now you have an assembly that should look like the one in this picture. First, break the fixture wires loose at each point where they cross the rim hoop. Then, as in the picture, clamp one end of a jig wire in a vise, grasp the hub tube between your fingers, and twist it to break the CA joint at the hub tube. Twist and pull to extract the jig wire from the assembly. Hold only the hub tube while doing this—not the rim. Repeat this with the other jig wires and clean the CA off the rim and the hub tube. Be careful not to cut any of the spokes. Clean out the insides of the axles with a drill bit, but use caution here: if the drill bit seizes, you might tear out your spokes.

5 Completing the rims. Position the other hoops on each side, jockey them around till you get the best fit, and clamp the rim and hoops together. Check to be sure the outside hoops are even with the center rim all around. Now run a thin coat of epoxy all the way around the outside, except at the clamp positions. When the epoxy sets, remove the clamps and epoxy the rest. Spray-paint the wheel lightly with silver, but not too much! You don't want your spokes to look as if they're made of scale barbed wire.

6 Now for the tires. The picture shows two versions: the bigger wheels use 1/2-inch-o.d., 1/16-inch-wall, black rubber tubing. I cut and lightly sand the ends to get a tight, clean joint; CA works great on this. Then a little epoxy works best to mount the tire on the rim. The finished, 3/8-inch-diameter wheels each weigh about 1 ounce. If your plane is heavier than 4 or 5 pounds, you may want to go with thicker, 1/8-inch-wall rubber tube tires.

For lighter wheels, I use the polyolefin foam "backer rod" used in caulking applications. It comes in diameters of 3/8 inch to 7/8 inch and is extremely light—only a few grams per tire. Using it alone as a tire, however, presents some problems: some brands are of such a light density that they can't be looped into a circle without folding; so you must find the dense stuff. Also, it is gray and just sloughs off paint and dye. I have found, however, that the rubber coating that tool handles are dipped in can be troweled on as an outside coat. If you can't find black, go ahead with red or blue and then color it with a black, felt-tip marker. Also, CA won't work to join this stuff; you must use epoxy. The smaller wheels in the picture show these foam tires without the rubberized coating. Complete with tires, these wheels each weigh less than 1 ounce and have withstood many a hard landing. ✦

Make a simple wheel-pant attachment
by Stan Alexander

Sometimes, the best way to do things is also the simplest. I like this technique my friend, Gary Parenti, developed to attach wheel pants to his impressive, ¼-scale Benes Mráz BE-50 Beta Minor. Gary uses rubber bands to hold the wheel pants firmly in place under his model's wings. This technique makes pants removal quick and easy, and it doesn't detract from the model's scale appearance. The photos and the illustrations show how it's done.

Gary's 106-inch-span model just wouldn't look right without its distinctive wheel pants. Using rubber bands to hold them in place is easy and uncomplicated. The technique can be used on many scale models.

A closeup of the pants shows the clean appearance of the wheel with pants attached to the wing. No screws were used.

Simple wheel-pant attachment
by Gary Parenti

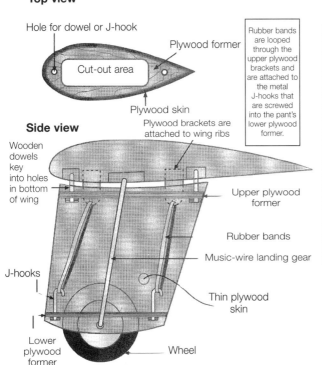

Top view

Hole for dowel or J-hook

Cut-out area

Plywood former

Plywood skin

Rubber bands are looped through the upper plywood brackets and are attached to the metal J-hooks that are screwed into the pant's lower plywood former.

Side view

Wooden dowels key into holes in bottom of wing

Plywood brackets are attached to wing ribs

Upper plywood former

Rubber bands

Music-wire landing gear

Thin plywood skin

J-hooks

Lower plywood former

Wheel

Simply pulling the pants downward reveals the rubber bands that are used to hold them in place. A couple of hooks secure the ends of the rubber bands; two wooden dowels key into holes in the wing's lower surface and hold the pants in position. The landing gear is simply a piece of bent music wire. ✦

Index of Manufacturers

Aeroloft
7919 E. Mawson Rd., Mesa, AZ 85207;
(602) 649-8662; fax (602) 649-8649;
www.aeroloft.com.

Aeroplane Works
2134 Gilbride Rd., Martinsville, NJ
08836; (908) 356-8557.

Aerospace Composite Products
14210 Doolittle Dr., San Leandro, CA
94577; www.acp-composites.com.

Aveox Electric Flight Systems
31324 Via Colinas, #103, Westlake
Village, CA 91362; (818) 597-8915; fax
(818) 597-0617.

Badger Air-Brush Co.
9128 W. Belmont Ave., Franklin Park, IL
60131; (847) 678-3104.

Balsa USA
P.O. Box 164, Marinette, WI 54143; (906)
863-6421; fax (906) 863-5878.

Balsarite by Coverite
distributed by Great Planes
(address below).

Bob Banka's Scale Model Research
3114 Yukon Ave., Costa Mesa, CA 92626;
(714) 979-8058.

Bob Dively Model Aircraft
38131 Airport Pky.#206, Willoughby, OH
44094; (216) 953-9254;
fax (216) 953-9311.

Bob Violett Models (BVM)
170 State Rd. 419; Winter Springs, FL
32708; (407) 327-6333; fax (407)
327-5020; www.bvmjets.com.

C.B. Tatone Inc.
21658 Cloud Way, Hayward, CA 94545;
(510) 783-4868; fax (510) 783-3283.

Carl Goldberg Models
4734 W. Chicago Ave., Chicago, IL
60651; (773) 626-9550;
fax (773) 626-9566.

Composite Structures Technology
P.O. Box 642, Tehachapi, CA 93581-0642;
(805) 822-4162.

Coverite
distributed by Great Planes
(address below).

Dave's Aircraft Works
34455 Camino El Molino, Capistrano
Beach, CA 92624; (949) 248-2773;
www.davesaircraftworks.com.

Dremel Tool
4915 21st St., Racine, WI 53406; (414)
554-1390; fax (414) 554-7654.

Du-Bro Products
P.O. Box 815, Wauconda, IL 60084; (800)
848-9411; fax (847) 526-1604;
www.dubro.com.

E-Z Lam
distributed by Aerospace Composite
Products (address above).

F&M Enterprises
22522 Auburn Dr., El Toro, CA 92630;
(714) 583-1455; fax (714) 583-1455.

Foley Mfg.
P.O. Box 245, Roanoke Rapids, NC 27870;
(919) 537-5237.

Hobby Lobby Intl.
5614 Franklin Pike Cir., Brentwood, TN
37027; (615) 373-1444; fax (615)
377-6948; www.hobby-lobby.com.

Hobby Poxy
36 Pine St., Rockaway, NJ 07866; (973)
625-3100; fax (973) 625-8303.

Ikon N'West
3806 Chase Rd., Post Falls, ID 83877;
(208) 773-9001.

Innovative Model Products (IMP)
P.O. Box 333, Remsen, NY 13438-0333;
(315) 831-2705; fax (315) 831-2805.

Innovative Products
P.O. Box 4365, Margate, FL 33063.

K&B Mfg. Inc.
2100 College Dr., Lake Havasu City, AZ
86403; (520) 453-3030;
fax (520) 453-3559.

K&S Engineering
6917 W. 59th St., Chicago, IL 60638;
(773) 586-8503.

K.J. Miller Corp.
22711 County Rd. 14, Elkhart, IN 46515.

Leading Edge Technologies
2438 Cedar Ave., White Bear Lake, MN
55110; (708) 771-2989.

Micro Fasteners
110 Hillcrest Rd., Flemington, NJ 08822;
(908) 806-4050; fax (908) 788-2607.

Model Magic
distributed by Leading Edge Technologies
(address above).

MonoKote
distributed by Great Planes
(address above).

Nick Ziroli Plans
29 Edgar Dr., Smithtown, NY11787; (516)
467-4765; fax (516) 467-1752.

O.S.
distributed by Great Planes;
www.osengines.com.

Oracover
distributed by Hobby Lobby Intl.
(address above).

Pacer Technology
9420 Santa Anita Ave., Rancho
Cucamonga, CA 91730; (909) 987-0550;
(800) 538-3091.

Partall Paste/Rexco
P.O. Box 1045, Carpinteria, CA 93013;
(805) 963-6505.

PFM
distributed by Innovative Products
(address above).

Pica
2655 N.E. 188th St., Miami, FL 33180.

Prather Products
1660 Ravenna Ave., Wilmington, CA
90744-1398; (310) 835-4764.

RAm (Radio Controlled Models)
229 E. Rollins Rd., Round Lake Beach, IL
60073; (847) 740-8726;
fax (847) 740-8727.

Randolph Products
P.O. Box 830, Carlstadt, NJ 07072-0830.

Robbe Model Sport
distributed by Aveox Electric Flight
Systems (address above).

Saito
4105 Fieldstone Rd., Champaign, IL
61821; (217) 355-9511;
www.horizonhobby.com.

Sig Mfg. Co. Inc.
P.O. Box 520, Montezuma, IA 50171;
(800) 247-5008; (515) 623-5154; fax (515)
623-3922; www.sigmfg.com.

Squadron/Signal Publications Inc.
1115 Crowley, Carrollton, TX 75011-
5010; (214) 242-1485;
fax (214) 242-3775.

Sullivan Products
P.O. Box 5166, Baltimore, MD 21224;
(410) 732-3500; fax (410) 327-7443.

Testor Corp.
620 Buckbee St., Rockford, IL 61104;
(815) 962-6654; fax (815) 962-7401.

Vortac Mfg. Co. Inc.
P.O. Box 469, Oak Lawn, IL 60453;
(708) 425-5885.

West System
distributed by Composite Structures
Technology (address above).

Williams Bros.
181 Pawnee St., San Marcos, CA 92069.

Zap Glue
9420 Santa Anita Ave., Rancho
Cucamonga, CA 91730.

Z-Poxy
distributed by Zap Glue (address above).

Ziroli
see Nick Ziroli.